HEALTH ECONOMICS:
AN INTRODUCTION TO
ECONOMIC EVALUATION
Second Edition

Gisela Kobelt

Office of Health Economics
12 Whitehall London SW1A 2DY
www.ohe.org

© March 2002. Office of Health Economics. Price £5.00

ISBN 1 899040 22 6

Printed by BSC Print Ltd, London.

About the Author

Gisela Kobelt is managing director of Health Dynamics International Ltd, a consulting company specializing in economic evaluation of health interventions and training courses in health economics. In addition, she is course director for the Strategic Health Economics Programme at the Stockholm School of Economics.

Previously she created and headed the Corporate Health Economics Departments at Pharmacia & Upjohn (Stockholm, Sweden and London, UK) and at Sandoz (Basel, Switzerland). Prior to her responsibilities with Sandoz, she was director of Human Resources, Finance and Administration at the Strasbourg Research Center of Merrell Dow for six years. She holds a Master's Degree from the University of Strasbourg in France and an MBA from the Institute for Management Development in Lausanne, Switzerland.

Acknowledgements

My heartfelt thanks go to Clive Pritchard of the Office of Health Economics, without whose editorial skills and input this revised edition would not have been possible. I am also grateful to Professor Bengt Jönsson of the Stockholm School of Economics and to the OHE reviewers for their advice and helpful comments on the manuscript.

The Second Edition

This second edition of 'Health Economics' has been updated to take account of methodological developments in the field of economic evaluation in health care and includes a number of detailed case studies which did not appear in the first edition.

OFFICE OF HEALTH ECONOMICS

CONTENTS

Foreword to the Second Edition

The second edition of this guide to economic evaluation is significantly extended. This mirrors the development of economic evaluation since the first edition was published in 1996. The methodology has developed and new techniques, both regarding costing and outcome measurement, have been introduced. Some concepts have, with the same arguments, been deleted or reduced in importance. The application of economic evaluation in decision-making has also taken a step forward. This is manifested in the inclusion of a section on NICE. The opportunities as well as the problems of using economic evaluations for administrative decisions are similar in other countries, even if the legal and institutional frameworks may differ.

But the main feature of this introduction to economic evaluation is still the use of practical examples to show how the techniques can be applied in different types of studies. The examples are no longer always simple, which reflects the development of methodology and application. But they provide an often-ignored lesson for the application of economic evaluation in health economics as well as in other fields. Knowledge of the techniques is important, but it is as important to be able to recognise which technique or method can and should be used for a specific assessment problem.

We are therefore sure that this revised and extended version will continue to provide an excellent introduction to economic evaluation, and at the same time stimulate the reader to further studies.

BENGT JÖNSSON
Professor of Health Economics, Stockholm School of Economics
ADRIAN TOWSE
Director of the Office of Health Economics

1 Health Economics – General Issues

1.1 The economics of health and health care

Over the past decades, our ability to provide treatments has increased exponentially with the introduction of new technologies, while at the same time the demand for health care has risen. As a natural consequence, health care costs have been and are increasing, putting a considerable strain on our finite health care resources.

Health economics (see Box 1) is now a term commonly used in public policy documents, in the medical and scientific literature, and in the lay press. This is one of the very visible signs of a quite dramatic change in the health care market. Attention is shifting from the 'passive' funding and administration of systems, in which physicians identify and provide appropriate care, to concerns about the resource costs of care and the health outcomes achieved from providing care. Economic questions are increasingly being addressed; how much should we spend on health care, and how do we ensure it is spent efficiently?

The aim of this guide is to provide a basic introduction to the methods of economic evaluation which have been developed to address this question. The current chapter provides some background to the issue, illustrating an increased level of interest in the use of economics by policy makers with examples of economic evaluation being formally incorporated into the decision making process in health care. Chapter two introduces the different types of economic evaluation and discusses the various ways in which analysts have approached the two components of this form of evaluation: how much does treatment cost and what effect does it have on health? Costing issues are illustrated with examples of a different types of analysis, the cost of illness study, which is merely concerned with the aggregate costs of treating a disease. Chapter three considers the methods of economic evaluation in more detail, focusing particularly on the use of modelling techniques which synthesise data from a range of sources. The chapter illustrates the use of these techniques with a number of examples (primarily of drug evaluations) and discusses the key areas of methodology to be considered when undertaking an economic analysis. Chapter four presents two examples of sets of methodological guidelines for the conduct of economic evaluation and chapter five concludes.

To put the discussion into context, total health care spending in the European Union ranges between around 7 and 11% of gross domestic product (GDP). After rising rapidly in the 1970s from around 5% of GDP, expenditures remained at a relatively stable percentage during the eighties, but started to grow again in the nineties, contributing to purchasers' demands to contain expenditures. As shown in Table 1, UK health care expenditure, as a

Box 1 A definition of health economics

'Health economics' can be defined as the application of the theories, tools and concepts of economics as a discipline to the topics of health and health care. Since economics as a science is concerned with the allocation of scarce resources, health economics is concerned with issues relating to the allocation of scarce resources to improve health. This includes both resource allocation within the economy to the health care system and within the health care system to different activities and individuals.

percentage of GDP, has consistently been at a lower level than the average for all European countries.

In Japan, the general trend has been similar, although starting from a lower percentage level than the other OECD countries. Contrary to this, US expenditure as a share of GDP has consistently been higher, and grown at a faster rate, than that of other OECD countries. There are several reasons for this difference of the US compared with Europe, one of the most important being that price levels for most medical services are comparatively high in the US and have been growing rapidly due to the traditional dominance of employer funded 'fee-for-service' private insurance. In response to this, there has been a shift to 'managed care' in the past decade, and a large and increasing part of the population is enrolled in managed care organizations (MCOs). While this has led to a reduced growth of health care expenditures, it appears currently that the cost-management measures by MCOs are perceived as too restrictive and new forms of health insurance models are emerging.

Numerous interacting factors contribute to increased health care costs, as indicated in Figure 1. Usually the first factor that comes to mind in the industrialised world is the growing elderly population with needs for both long term medical and social care. The population over 65 years of age consumes a substantial share of health care resources. However, it is not the increase in

Table 1 Health care expenditures as percentage of gross domestic product

Country	1970	1980	1990	1998
United States	6.9	8.7	11.9	12.9
Japan	4.6	6.5	6.1	7.4
European Union	5.0	7.3	7.8	8.6
UK	4.5	5.3	5.7	6.8
OECD average	5.8	7.3	8.7	9.9

Source: OECD health data 2001

Figure 1 **Major contributors to the growth of health care costs**

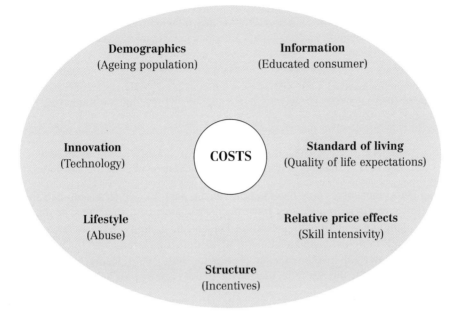

numbers of any of the population groups per se, but our willingness and ability to provide much more care which is pushing up health care expenditures. Indeed the major driver of the cost increase is the availability of an increased number of treatment options and our adoption of continuous improvements in the quality and intensity of care. Although productivity has increased in the delivery of health care as a consequence of programmes to increase efficiency, the health care sector is labour and skill intensive compared to other sectors and will hence always lag behind the average of the economy.

In Europe, concerns about the financing of health care are high on every government's agenda, as health care is predominantly financed with public money, either by taxes, by social insurance or a combination of both. The figures are shown in Table 2.

It is unavoidable that choices and trade-offs have to be made, as there will always be more treatment options than the resources will allow. Mostly, and certainly in Europe, these choices involve public decisions about allocation of resources within a fixed budget, and replacing old treatments with newer ones will have to be based on formal evaluations of whether the additional health benefit (effectiveness) is worth the additional cost.

Governments in Europe have attempted to contain costs, with a variety of measures aimed at both the demand for and the supply of health care. In the case of the prescription pharmaceutical market a large spectrum of economic

Table 2 **Public health expenditures as percent of total health expenditures**

Country	1970	1980	1990	1998
United States	36	42	40	45
Japan	70	71	78	79
European Union	77	78	76	76
UK	87	89	88	83
OECD average	53	62	59	60

Source: OECD health data 2001

regulation measures have been applied in the past decade as set out in Table 3. However, these regulations have been less successful than was hoped in controlling the growth of expenditure. They have, in many cases, also created additional complexity and economic distortion, often ignoring the need to create an overall health care environment that would foster appropriate responsibility for the cost-effective use of health care by purchasers, providers and patients.

Payers for health and care, particularly in Europe but also in the US, are therefore now looking more and more for value for money from health care

Table 3 **Some examples of cost containment measures for prescription drugs in Europe**

Type of regulation	Countries applicable
Price cuts, price freezes	across Europe
Reference pricing	Germany, Netherlands, Sweden, Spain, Portugal, Norway
Positive or negative lists	across Europe
De-listings	e.g. UK, Italy, Spain, France
Increased patient co-payment	across Europe
Greater use of generics	e.g. UK, Germany, Netherlands, Spain, France
Prescribing budgets for doctors	e.g. Germany, UK
Reductions in wholesaler and retail pharmacy margins	e.g. Netherlands
Lower promotional budget limits	e.g. France
Profit limits	e.g. UK
Volume contracts	e.g. France

Box 2 **Assessment criteria for new therapies**

Efficacy:	Does it work in a controlled environment (clinical trials)?
Safety:	Does it have side effects and are these acceptable and manageable?
Effectiveness:	Does it work in the normal environment?
Cost-effectiveness:	Is it an efficient use of resources?

interventions, in an effort to attain the desired goal i.e. the best possible health and health care within available resources. This represents a further fundamental change of attitude to health care. We have moved firstly, away from technology and provider-driven development to a very cost conscious environment, and now from a concern about cost alone to one of cost-effectiveness. Innovative therapies, be they medicines or other interventions, are being assessed for both effectiveness and cost-effectiveness, rather than only for efficacy and safety (see Box 2). Their acceptability will be more explicitly related to the cost and value of the incremental improvement they bring to the patient.

1.2 The role of health economic evaluation studies

Since value for money is now of central concern in health policy, analyses of the consequences of the use of new and existing therapies, both in terms of benefits and costs, are crucial for decisions on resource allocation. Purchasers of health care are increasingly requesting proof of the value for money of competing technologies, in particular of new pharmaceutical products, in order to decide on their adoption and reimbursement status, and cost-effectiveness has become an important criterion for selection of therapies by providers and payers of health care.

Economic evaluations have therefore become an important source of information to aid decision making about the allocation of resources to technologies, and also to decisions about the development of new pharmaceuticals and medical devices. In most countries, there are specialized groups within governments who assess current and new technologies in health care, and economic evaluations are an integral part of such assessments. An economic evaluation is a tool to assess the benefits and the costs of different uses of scarce resources.

As defined in Box 3, an economic evaluation provides a comparative analysis of alternative courses of action, in terms of their costs and consequences. This entails comparing different treatment strategies over the entire course of a disease or defined disease episodes in order to decide upon the best option for different patient groups, given the expected costs. Such evaluations use aggregate measurements and will provide information for groups of patients

Box 3 Definition and forms of economic evaluation

A comparative analysis of two or more options in terms of their costs and consequences:

Cost consequences analysis (CCA)
Cost-minimization analysis (CMA)
Cost-effectiveness analysis (CEA)
Cost-utility analysis (CUA)
Cost-benefit analysis (CBA)

rather than individuals. Whilst there are different techniques to measure consequences, depending on the disease or the desired goal, all evaluations use similar techniques to estimate costs.

It should be borne in mind when analyzing costs that they can be incurred by a number of different parties and that it is desirable for all costs to be included for a relevant time period, regardless of the fact that they are often falling on different budgets within the health care system. For instance, a new treatment may increase the pharmaceutical budget, but it may, over time, produce savings in other parts of the system, such as lower hospitalization costs and fewer monitoring requirements, that may partly or fully offset this increase. Also, savings may occur in other sectors of the economy, if for instance absenteeism is reduced, or premature deaths avoided. For efficient resource allocation, health care decision makers need to look at total costs of therapies over a given time. Where the more costly of two mutually exclusive alternative treatments, A and B, is also the more effective, then an incremental cost-effectiveness ratio may be calculated (see Box 4). The more costly intervention is preferred if the incremental cost per unit of health effect is less than the decision maker's willingness to pay for health gains.

The potential benefit of using health economic evaluations is quite obvious, and health care decision makers are starting to integrate them into their

Box 4 Definition of the incremental cost-effectiveness ratio (ICER)

$$\frac{[\text{ Cost (B) } - \text{ Cost (A) }]}{[\text{ Effect (B) } - \text{ Effect (A) }]} \quad \text{or} \quad \frac{\text{Difference in Cost}}{\text{Difference in Effect}}$$

Where B is more effective and more expensive than A.

(If B is more effective and less expensive than A, it dominates A and the ICER is not calculated.)

Table 4 **Actual/potential use of pharmacoeconomic data by European authorities**

Country	Price negotiation	Deciding on reimbursement	Deciding on local formulary inclusion
Belgium	–	+	+
Denmark	–	+	+
Finland	+	+	–
France	+	+	–
Germany	–	–	+
Italy	–	+	–
The Netherlands	–	+	+
Norway	+	+	–
Portugal	–	+	–
Spain	–	+	–
Sweden	+	+	+
Switzerland	+	+	–
UK	–	–	+

Symbols: + Economic data could be or have been used
     – Economic data are not required

Source: Adapted from Drummond et al. 1999

decision making processes. Two international studies (Drummond et al. 1993 and 1999) investigated the actual and potential use of pharmacoeconomics and outcomes research by authorities in Europe (Table 4). During the years between these two studies, the use of these techniques has become much more widespread, as such studies provide part of the basis upon which certain pricing and reimbursement authorities or formulary committees make decisions. But they may also show to individual practitioners and pharmacists what the overall consequences, financial and other, of their prescribing and dispensing are. They are, however, not an official part of the scientific approval and market authorization of new products.

1.2.1 Official requirements for economic evaluation

The increasing importance of the assessment of medical technology for health policy, and of economic evaluation of new treatments for decisions about their adoption, may be viewed against the background of the large number of such studies that have been performed during the past decade (see Figure 2). These factors have led to the development of a number of guidelines for the conduct and the methodology of economic evaluations.

Overall, such guidelines fall into three different categories:

Figure 2 **Growth in the economic evaluations literature – applied studies**

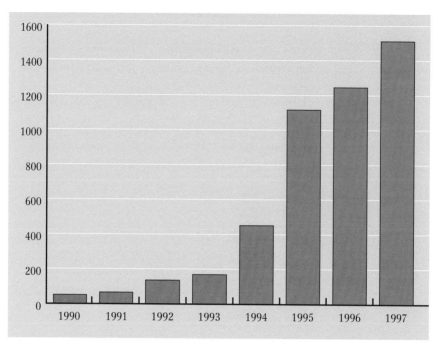

Source: OHE Health Economic Evaluations Database (HEED) September 2001
Applied studies are original evaluations and include those studies listed in Box 3, cost
analyses and cost of illness studies.

- reimbursement guidelines, i.e. guidelines issued by authorities that make
  the submission of economic evaluations mandatory for listing a new
  product on the reimbursement formulary;

- methodological guidelines, i.e. guidelines proposed by researchers or
  groups of researchers with the aim of improving the techniques and
  methods used and to make studies more transparent;

- guidelines on researcher independence, i.e. guidelines that attempt to deal
  with problems of bias in such studies.

The first country to make submission of economic studies an official
requirement for listing medicines on the national drug formulary for
reimbursement was Australia in 1993 (Commonwealth of Australia:
Department of Human Services and Health, 1995). After a few years'
experience, the guidelines were revised and updated. The next to follow was
Canada, based on an initiative in Ontario later picked up by British Columbia.
In addition, methodological guidelines elaborated together with all
stakeholders – government, insurance companies, providers' associations
(hospitals, pharmacists, physicians), academia and industry – were published
in 1994 (Canadian Coordinating Office for Health Technology Assessment,

1994), a revised edition of which was published in 1997. These latter guidelines are widely considered to be authoritative in terms of methodological standards and most of the documents published subsequently have relied heavily on the Canadian document.

Initially, European countries had taken a somewhat different approach. While guidelines as an expression of methodological standards were elaborated and published in most countries, they were not used at first to support a reimbursement requirement. Now, however, a number of countries have made economic evaluation mandatory for reimbursement decisions (see Table 5). In addition, in many other countries, the submission of economic evaluations is encouraged or expected.

Among those countries where economic analysis must be considered prior to deciding on reimbursement, Australia, Canada and New Zealand are the most long standing and the most extensive users of the requirement. Like their antipodean counterparts, the authorities in the provinces of Ontario and British Columbia (BC) require an economic submission with every claim for a new drug to be placed on the publicly reimbursed formulary. Although there is little published information on submissions to these bodies, George et al. (2001) report on 355 submissions to the Australian Pharmaceutical Benefits Advisory Committee (PBAC) made between January 1991 and June 1996 and Anis and Gagnon (2000) have reviewed 95 applications for formulary inclusion under British Columbia's drug plan between January 1996 and April 1999. Elsewhere, there are differences in the extent to which economic analysis is or will be used. In the UK, the National Institute for Clinical Excellence (see section 1.2.2) assesses the value for money of only a sample of new and existing technologies, and the public reimbursement of new drugs has not been made conditional on cost-effectiveness. The powers which the Portuguese and Danish authorities have to base reimbursement decisions on cost-effectiveness are not used systematically, while the Dutch authorities intend to apply an economic criterion to reimbursement decisions only for drugs which cannot be included in an existing therapeutic cluster under the reference pricing scheme.

Overall, guidelines developed in different countries differ very little from one another, which can be seen as an expression of a general consensus about what constitutes acceptable methodology. Differences relate basically to the acceptance of modelling studies, the type of costs to be included or excluded, the discount rate and the level of detail relating to forecasts of usage of the new product. As most of the countries that have made these studies mandatory are rather small, they all agree in their acceptance of the results of studies transferred and adapted from other countries.

In the US, the Department of Health and Human Services commissioned a panel of academic experts, the 'Washington Panel', to elaborate a set of guidelines for good practice. The effort has resulted in a widely quoted book (Gold et al., 1996) that has also sparked intense scientific discussion aimed at

Table 5 **Guidelines for economic evaluation**

Country	Observations
Formal guidelines	
Australia	Mandatory requirement for all new drugs since 1993
Canada (British Columbia)	Mandatory requirement for all new drugs since 1996
Canada (Ontario)	Mandatory requirement for all new drugs since 1995
Denmark	Can be requested (since 1997) or submitted voluntarily
Finland	Mandatory requirement for all new drugs since 1998
France	Power to request since 1997
Italy	Power to request since 1998
The Netherlands	Mandatory requirement from 2003 (test phase since 1998)
New Zealand	Mandatory requirement for all new drugs since 1993
Norway	Mandatory requirement for all new drugs from 2002 (test phase since 2000)
Portugal	Power to request since 1999
UK (England and Wales)	Submissions invited from companies by the National Institute for Clinical Excellence (NICE) for some new and established drugs and devices since 1999
USA	Mandatory requirements by two Health Maintenance Organizations (HMOs) operating in Arizona and Colorado
Informal guidelines	
France	Guidelines by the Syndicat National de l'Industrie Pharmaceutique (SNIP) and researchers
Germany	Guidelines proposed by researchers
Italy	Guidelines proposed by researchers
Spain	Guidelines proposed by researchers
Sweden	No guidelines – but regular use
UK	Informal guidelines (Department of Health/ Association of the British Pharmaceutical Industry) superceded by NICE
USA	Methodological guidelines by the Panel on Cost-Effectiveness in Health and Medicine convened by the US Public Health Service (Gold et al., 1996) Guidelines published by the pharmaceutical industry association, the Pharmaceutical Research and Manufacturers of America (PhRMA)

further development of the methods. Examples of issues which have attracted attention are whether costs and health effects should be discounted at the same rate and whether some quality of life measures capture the impact of time off work due to illness. A similar effort to promote good methodology was also undertaken in Europe, spearheaded by academic researchers and supported by the European Community (Graf von der Schulenburg, 2000).

A quite different initiative has also been taken in the US, led by a group of academic researchers, in order to define guidelines to avoid potential bias in the conduct of economic evaluations. Their suggestion is that such evaluations ought only to be performed by independent researchers with no direct financial link to the sponsor (Task Force on Principles for Economic Analysis of Health Care Technology, 1995), or if a study is sponsored, researchers should have complete freedom to publish any results. There is a legitimate concern that, unlike the procedure for clinical trials, protocols for economic evaluations of new drugs are not always defined up-front, thereby allowing modification of, for example, the effectiveness measures and analytical methods used at a later stage. However, the solution to such potential problems may lie in adherence to good practices by all participants in this evolving field rather than in contractual arrangements. The more precise the research question, the better the methodology and the relevance of the data used in the study, the more complete and transparent the reporting of the results, the more credible will be the claims for value for money and the more useful will the studies be for decision making. The Canadian (Ontario) guidelines, for example, request that all steps in the study be described, starting with a simple cost analysis, before moving on to the more complex comparisons. They also recommend contractual arrangements between investigators and sponsors establishing the investigators' independence with regard to methods and reporting of results. The best way to reduce doubts regarding potential bias and permit objective assessment of the quality of a study is, however, good methodology and transparency as to how the results have been arrived at plus complete and timely publication of findings and comprehensive disclosure of sources of funding.

The United Kingdom, like other countries, has followed its own road, combining health technology assessment and clinical guidance. The National Institute for Clinical Excellence (NICE) was set up in 1999 by the Department of Health in order to assess existing and new pharmaceutical and other medical technologies and recommend whether and how they should be used within the English and Welsh National Health Service (NHS).

1.2.2 NICE
The objectives of NICE are to:

- help to promote faster access to the best treatments, and to new treatments which offer real benefits to patients;

- help to end the lottery of "post-code prescribing". Patients will be clear about which treatments are recommended for routine use in the NHS, and which are still experimental or only suitable in certain circumstances;

- help the NHS to deliver the best possible health care from available resources, by focusing on the most cost-effective treatments.

NICE's role is therefore to promote the use of cost-effective treatments in England and Wales with the aim of ensuring that the availability of these treatments does not vary by region, or postcode. It is expected that "guidance from NICE will lead to greater equity of access to effective treatments across the NHS" (Department of Health, 1999). Part of NICE's work (and the most significant component to date) is a programme of technology appraisals. Technologies are referred to NICE by the Department of Health and the National Assembly of Wales using one or more of the following criteria:

- Is the technology likely to result in a significant health benefit, across the NHS as a whole, if given to all relevant patients?

- Is the technology likely to have a significant impact on other health-related government policies, such as reduction in health inequalities?

- Is the technology likely to have a significant impact on NHS resources (financial or other) if given to all relevant patients?

- Is NICE likely to be able to add value by issuing national guidance? For instance, might there otherwise be controversy over the available evidence on clinical and cost-effectiveness?

Under the technology appraisals programme, NICE's role is "to appraise the clinical benefits and the costs of such healthcare interventions as may be notified by the Secretary of State or the National Assembly of Wales and to make recommendations" (NICE, 2000). NICE commissions one of a handful of academic groups to review the existing evidence on each technology and, for drugs, new evidence contained in the manufacturer's submission. Companies are not compelled to provide evidence, and the appraisal would still proceed without it, but so far company submissions have been received for all drug appraisals. A summary version of the guidance which has been developed for the content of company submissions is presented in section 4 towards the end of this book.

Unlike systems put in place in other countries, NICE does not represent a complete barrier to a drug being publicly reimbursed; an individual clinician can prescribe a drug on the NHS even if NICE has recommended against its use. However, since the beginning of 2002, it has been obligatory for health authorities to fund prescriptions based on NICE recommendations. Other differences with systems elsewhere are that NICE appraises both drug and non-drug technologies and that, of the drugs appraised, many are established rather than newly marketed pharmaceuticals. Of the first 28 full appraisals completed, 18 were of pharmaceuticals and only one of these took place prior to the medicine's UK launch.

In common with other jurisdictions (e.g. Australia, New Zealand, British Columbia), NICE has recommended that the use of some drugs be restricted to a narrower group of patients than that for which the drug is licensed. Of the recommendations arising from the first 18 drug appraisals, 11 were of this type. It is unusual for a drug to be rejected outright, the only example during this period being the separate rapid appraisal of Relenza (a decision partially reversed by the subsequent full appraisal).

NICE was, at inception, conceived by many to be an instrument of cost control but, according to NICE's estimates of the cost impact of its technology appraisals to the end of 2001, the annual cost to the English and Welsh NHS could be as much as £200 million. However, some of NICE's positive recommendations have proved controversial and there was evidence that local decision makers were unwilling to devote additional resources to implementing NICE guidance, though this is now mandatory. The impact of NICE on clinical practice and on health care costs is therefore difficult to evaluate. Where NICE has unambiguously succeeded has been in furthering the debate about the appropriateness of different types of data and their timing when attempting to estimate the cost-effectiveness of pharmaceuticals. Even when a drug has been established for some time, the evidence base can be dominated by (clinical) studies conducted prior to launch. The establishment of NICE has reinforced once again the need for the pharmaceutical and medical device industry to address cost-effectiveness concerns during the development phase.

1.3 The importance of economic evaluations for the development of new technologies

Pharmaceutical companies have long performed economic evaluations at the time of launch of a new product. Today, in most pharmaceutical companies, these studies are an integral part of research portfolio management and drug development in order to bring products to the market that meet customers' goal of value for money. With the establishment of a mandatory requirement in many countries, economic evaluations have, however, ceased to be simply a marketing tool to provide information for customers. Rather, their focus has changed to support reimbursement decisions, with the risk that once these decisions have been made (to list or not to list on the formulary), there has been less concern with ensuring that drugs are used efficiently. As large efforts are made to perform evaluations when a product is first introduced, based on limited information, resources are often not available to continue these efforts beyond the time of the launch, in order to continuously provide relevant information on how products and therapies can best be used. NICE, and its mandate to evaluate treatments that have been in the market for some time, may encourage companies to make efforts during the entire lifespan of a treatment, particularly if they are expected to have a favourable influence on NICE's re-assessments of previously appraised technologies. Similarly, some countries' intention to review reimbursement decisions once a treatment has been used for some time may provide incentives to perform more studies that will ultimately support efforts to improve efficiency in health care provision.

It is not easy to decide when the best time for an economic evaluation is. Prior to launch, only experimental data are available, where efficacy is measured in a controlled environment and in well-defined patients and resource use is influenced by clinical protocols. Nevertheless, these are the only data available when decisions about reimbursements have to be made, and it appears more useful to have some supporting economic evidence available, albeit limited, rather than none – as decisions have to be made regardless. However, integrating this type of research into the development process and combining clinical and economic objectives presents a number of challenges, and some of these are:

- How can efficacy be translated into effectiveness?

- What is an appropriate outcome measure?

- What is an appropriate timeframe for the economic analysis, compared to the clinical proof of efficacy?

- What is the influence of stringent study protocols on outcome? On resource use?

- What is the appropriate comparison? (Guidelines variously require the most used and the least costly alternative treatment.) And how can one deal with comparisons against placebo?

Some of these points are addressed in the methodological guidelines, but very often the decision of what needs to be done is heavily influenced by what can be done, rather than what ideally should be done, given the timeframe, the resource constraints, the data availability and the indication studied. Hence, no general rules can be made, but the overall combination of clinical and economic development is illustrated in Figures 3 and 4.

Figure 3 **Elaboration of documentation of value for money**

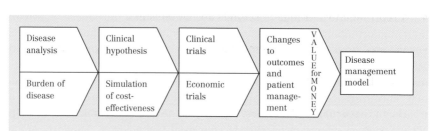

Figure 4 **Workflow of economic evaluation within the development process**

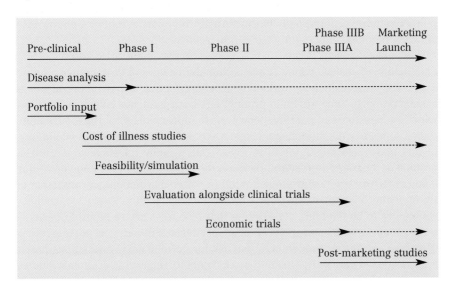

The process spans the full development time of new products and will be more successful if performed with regard to the anticipated information needs of providers and payers and if fully integrated into the clinical development process (Figure 3). In the earlier stages of development, activities will involve largely desk work and basic research about the disease, its economic consequences and the costs of treatments. In later stages, economic trials are often carried out alongside phase III clinical trials because at this stage of the development process the product being evaluated is in the state in which it will be launched. The resource data collected during the trial will then be used to evaluate the cost-effectiveness of the product within the trial, but also complemented with data from other sources to model different time frames. In some cases, naturalistic studies (i.e. studies where the influence of the study protocol is minimal) will be conducted in order to assess the economic impact of a treatment. Naturalistic studies are characterised by (Buxton et al., 1997):

- Patients typical of the normal caseload;

- Comparison of the treatment under investigation with usual care;

- A representative sample of settings and physicians;

- Absence of blinding to treatment given (by physicians or patients);

- The following of patients under routine conditions;

- The measurement of a range of endpoints such as efficacy, feasibility, tolerance, quality of life, resource use.

Such studies are rather infrequent, as they are difficult to perform for practical and ethical reasons, or cannot be performed within the time limits imposed by reimbursement negotiations. Thus, most of this work entails a compromise between the ideal study and what can be realistically done.

Conducting extensive economic evaluation at all stages of development can be expensive, and knowledge about the most effective use of a product will accumulate over time after the product has been launched and is being used with large numbers of patients. However, the incentives to perform economic evaluations after the launch of a product are rather few. Currently, evaluations in this phase are mostly done to investigate specific questions regarding a product or a patient population. However, as the flexibility to change prices for medical technology is extremely limited in some jurisdictions, for example in Europe, the investment in larger evaluations may often seem to producer companies to be too high, considering that resources are required to perform evaluations for the next generation of products. Should – as is sometimes discussed – requirements emerge that ask for proof of early evaluations based on clinical trial data only, linked to more flexibility in pricing, economic studies during marketing phases will become more frequent and provide valuable data about resource use in clinical practice.

One of the most difficult issues is for health care decision makers to know, and state explicitly, what the threshold of cost-effectiveness should be – where products and other treatments that fail to meet the hurdle would be excluded from reimbursement using public funds. A balance has therefore to be struck between the costs and benefits of preparing economic evaluations. There is no point in generating economic information that will not be used or which could be misleading. There is no doubt, however, that a good economic evaluation will provide useful information for decision makers interested in the cost-effectiveness of resource use in the health care system.

2 Forms of Health Economic Evaluations

2.1 Introduction

A health economic evaluation is a way of establishing the 'value for money' of different health care technologies. Taking as our starting point the definition given in Box 3 of an economic evaluation in health care as *"a comparative analysis of alternative courses of action in terms of both their costs and consequences"* [Drummond et al., 1997], economic analyses are always comparative and are applied to explicit alternatives. One pharmaceutical product can be compared with more or less of itself, or with another, or with another type of intervention such as surgery, or with a 'watchful waiting' approach, whereby a patient receives no form of medical intervention but is instead monitored for any change in health status. Thus, a treatment cannot be cost-effective by itself, but only in relation to one or several relevant alternatives, and for defined patient groups. Whatever the alternative, at a minimum all the costs related to each method of treating a disease episode must be considered and related to the benefits, in terms of improvement in the length or quality of life.

All forms of economic evaluation involve assessment of both the inputs (the use of resources) and the level of outputs (health benefits) of the health care programmes to be compared and so facilitate the process of choosing the most appropriate use for scarce resources. If a treatment strategy is both better and less costly, it dominates the alternatives. More often, however, a treatment strategy that is better will also be more expensive and, as was noted in section 1.2, a judgement will have to be made as to whether the *incremental benefit* is worth the *incremental cost*. The inputs, or costs, of a treatment are defined as the cost of administering and taking the treatment minus the costs that are avoided because of the treatment. While it is not always easy to identify, quantify and value the resources used or saved because of lack of detailed data, they are more likely to be plausibly expressed in monetary terms than the incremental benefit, and will therefore be comparable. Outputs are more difficult to estimate for several reasons. Treatments often have an effect on several different parameters, and it may not be obvious how to combine them into one comprehensive outcome measure. Figure 5 illustrates the structure of economic evaluations.

The INPUTS are defined as:

- *Direct costs*, i.e. costs related to the use of resources due to either the disease or its treatment. They include costs to the health care system, but also costs to social services and to patients themselves or to their relatives.

- *Indirect or productivity costs*, i.e. costs related to loss of production, due to either the disease or its treatment, which occur to society.

Figure 5 **Structure of economic evaluation**

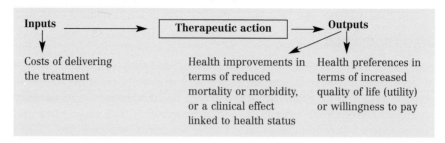

Other costs which may be influenced by treatment are:

- *Intangible costs*, i.e. costs related to suffering and the loss of quality of life due the disease or its treatment, which occur to the patient. These costs are particularly difficult to measure and value and, as a result, are often left out of any analysis. Current approaches used to assess intangible costs include the use of quality of life instruments, or direct measurements within the framework of willingness to pay assessments. In this way, intangible costs can be incorporated into the assessment of outcomes.

The OUTCOMES are measured as health improvements expressed as:

- *Disease measures* such as events avoided or delayed (e.g. hip fractures avoided in osteoporosis), patients successfully treated (e.g. number of patients in complete remission in cancer), etc.

- *Survival* measured as lives saved or life years saved.

- *Quality-adjusted survival* expressed as quality-adjusted life years (QALYs).

- *Monetary value*, expressed as willingness-to-pay for a benefit.

2.2 Types of economic evaluation

Economic evaluations can be categorised according to the types listed in Box 3. These are distinguished primarily by the way in which outcomes are treated. The appropriate means of evaluating outcomes will depend on a number of factors. The target audience, or the perspective for the study (i.e. whether it is a clinician selecting a treatment for a given group of patients or a policy maker wishing to set priorities between patient groups), the medical technology used and the availability of the data will play an important role. However, by far the most important factor is the medical and economic problem addressed, where the medical question will condition what effectiveness measure is used, while the economic question will influence both the effectiveness measure and the type of evaluation to be used. In general:

- if the economic question is whether a treatment is a good use of resources within the disease area, the comparison is with similar treatments and the outcome measure can be disease specific. The type of evaluation will be a cost-effectiveness analysis, if there is only a single outcome. With multiple outcomes, it is necessary to choose one, or to construct an index. For example, outcomes in hypertension can be stroke or chronic heart disease; in osteoporosis, several different types of fractures can happen and, in cancer, outcomes can be measured in terms of survival, remissions, side-effects, quality of life, etc.;

- if the economic question is whether a treatment represents a good investment considering the entire spectrum of diseases, the comparison will be with treatments in other diseases and the outcome measure will need to be generic, such as for instance the quality-adjusted life year (QALY), a combination of length of life and quality of life. This will give a cost-utility analysis, a specific type of cost-effectiveness analysis. The same type of analysis will also be appropriate when quality of life is an important component of the effect of a disease and its treatment.

By far the most important question to ask, however, before embarking on an economic evaluation is whether or not there is clear and well-documented clinical evidence for the technology to be compared to the available alternative(s). An economic evaluation can only be as good as the underlying effectiveness data, and the highest quality economic data will not be able to overcome any deficiency in the effectiveness data.

Table 6 summarizes the effectiveness measures used in the different types of analyses and indicates what questions each type of analysis can typically be used to address. Each of these analyses will be discussed in detail later in this chapter. A form of analysis we also discuss is the cost-of-illness study, which attempts to establish the economic burden that a particular disease or illness places upon society. Since these studies do not consider the outcomes of treatment, they are of limited value to decision makers concerned with achieving value for money in health care. However, they are often mentioned together with true economic evaluation studies as their findings may act as background data for economic analyses.

2.3 Cost data for economic evaluation

2.3.1 Steps in cost assessment

Assessing the costs in an economic evaluation involves four steps, and these steps are identical in all forms of evaluation:

1) identify the relevant resources used, regardless of whether they can be measured or not;

Table 6 **Effectiveness measures in different types of economic analyses and their use**

Analysis	Effectiveness measure	Potential use
Cost consequences analysis	Different disease specific measures, e.g. relapses avoided, myocardial infarctions avoided, etc.	Description of costs and of outcomes
Cost-minimization analysis	Not measured (assumes that the effects of alternatives are identical) or finds no difference in outcomes	Comparison of treatments within the same disease
Cost-effectiveness analysis	One disease specific measure (e.g. relapses avoided), patients with their illness controlled, disease-free time, a more general measure such as life years saved, or an index encompassing multiple measures	Comparison of treatments within the same disease
Cost-utility analysis	Summary measure combining survival and quality of life, e.g. quality-adjusted life years	Comparison of treatments for different diseases
Cost-benefit analysis	Effectiveness expressed as monetary benefit (e.g. willingness to pay)	Comparison of investments in the health care sector with investments in other sectors (e.g. education, road safety)

2) quantify these resources in physical units such as hospital days, surgical procedures, physician visits, tests, etc.;

3) value the different resources used at their opportunity costs. Ideally, unit costs will be applied to each different type of resource identified in 2), for example, using wage rates to value the time of health care professionals. Luce et al. (1996) recommend this 'micro costing' approach but argue that the need for precision in the cost estimates should be weighed against the difficulty and expense of acquiring the necessary information. At the other

end of the spectrum, in terms of level of detail, 'macro costing' uses cost estimates based on aggregate measures of resource use, such as an episode of hospitalization for a particular event;

4) deal with differential timing at which resource use can occur (discounting).

2.3.2 Perspectives

The first step involves a decision about the perspective from which the study is carried out, as this will drive what resources are relevant. The most frequently used perspectives are the societal perspective and the third party payer perspective. In the societal perspective, all costs, regardless of who incurs them, are included. Thus, costs to the health care service, to social services, to patients and also to the rest of society in the form of production losses are included, but transfer payments are ignored. Examples of transfer payments are taxes for health care consumption and reimbursements for income loss due to illness. For society as a whole, taxes and reimbursements represent a money flow from one part of society to another, but no resources (labour, capital) are being used up. The relevant concept of cost in economics is that of opportunity cost, meaning the benefit forgone from using resources for one purpose rather than in their best alternative use. This definition serves to remind us that costs will be incurred even when the use of a resource is not associated with any financial flows, such as in the case of a voluntary carer.

In the perspective of a third party payer, e.g. government, insurance company, managed care organization, only resources paid for by that organization are included. For instance, any reimbursements to patients for income loss are an actual cost to the third party payer. A good example of the effect of different perspectives is shown in Table 7, in a cost of illness study for multiple sclerosis.

Table 7 **Mean costs per patient for different perspectives in a cost of illness study of multiple sclerosis in Germany**

Costs	Cost per person and year (DM, 1999)	
	Societal perspective	Public payer perspective
Hospital inpatient care	6679	6255
Ambulatory care	4636	2527
Drugs	4596	4156
Services	8541	1452
Adaptations (investments)	5322	2687
Informal care	7917	–
Indirect costs	27830	–
Transfer costs (pensions)	–	7735
Total cost	65521	24812

Source: Kobelt et al, EFI report 399, 2000, Stockholm School of Economics, and Kobelt et al, HEPAC 2001, 2(2)

2.3.3 Resource quantification

In the second and third steps, a standard unit of resource consumption is defined, e.g. a hospital admission, a hospital day, a physician visit. Table 8 presents examples of the types of resources for which data are frequently collected. The quantity of the units used is then multiplied by the unit cost (price) to obtain the total cost.

2.3.4 Resource valuation

Bearing in mind the concept of opportunity cost introduced in section 2.3.2 as benefit forgone, a simple example of an opportunity cost is the cost of a physician's time during a visit. The time used during one consultation cannot be used for another consultation and hence has a cost. The opportunity cost in this case is the value lost for the consultation that was not undertaken.

In normal well-functioning markets, market prices are a good representation of the opportunity costs of resources, but in health care this is not always the case. In countries with a national health service, such as the UK or Sweden, resources may not be subject to market valuations. In some countries, the only easy source of costs is tariffs (i.e. prices set by a government or a public insurer for payment to health care providers such as hospitals or physicians) and although, for some resources, tariffs may represent the actual opportunity costs, for many they will not. In fee-for-service systems where each service is paid for individually, tariffs may be set to include incentives for the level of supply of a given resource, with high tariffs set to encourage provision and low tariffs to discourage it. An example of this issue can be seen in Table 9 in a cost of illness study in glaucoma. In other countries, the easiest available unit costs may be billings (charges) from providers to different payers, generally insurers or health plans. Often such charges may be used to subsidize other activities, e.g. within the hospital, and will hence be higher than the opportunity costs. This is the case for instance in the USA, where often a cost-charge ratio of 1:2 is applied.

There is also the question of applying appropriate valuations to those resources which have an opportunity cost, even if there is no market price, such as informal care by family members or friends. There is currently no general agreement on how to value these, and a decision has to be made whether they should be included or not, and if so, at what cost. Most often, a "replacement cost" is used, in this case the cost of a professional providing the care in lieu of the family, or alternatively the loss of leisure time due to providing care is valued as a fraction of the average national income. However, these costs do not necessarily have to be valued in monetary terms for decision makers to take them into account.

The role played by <u>indirect costs</u> (also termed productivity costs) will to some extent depend on the pathology being analysed. In diseases such as asthma, depression, schizophrenia, multiple sclerosis and migraine, indirect costs tend to be an important part of the total cost of the illness, because these diseases

Table 8 **Typical items of resource use in an economic evaluation**

Cost type	*Resources*
Direct medical costs	Hospitalization – days of hospitalization – discharges Outpatient visits – outpatient clinic attendance – visit to private practitioner – visit to paramedic Procedures and tests – tests (blood analysis, X-ray, ultrasound scans, gastroscopies, etc.) – surgical interventions Devices – medical devices (wheelchairs, hearing aid, pacemakers, etc.) Services – home care (hours or days) – nursing care (hours or days) Etc.
Direct non-medical costs	Transportation – for outpatient visits (ambulance, taxi, etc.) – for daily activities Services – home help (hours or days) – meals on wheels – social assistance (hours or days) Devices and investments – adaptation to house or car – special kitchen and bathroom utensils Informal care – care by relatives (is sometimes also considered an indirect cost) Etc.
Indirect costs	Sick leave (days or weeks) Reduced productivity at work (percentage or hours) Early retirement due to illness (years to normal retirement) Premature death (years to normal retirement)

affect age groups with a high labour force participation. In diseases that affect predominantly elderly people, indirect costs would be less important. There are different approaches to the valuation of indirect costs. In general, based on the human capital theory, the production of an individual is considered at

Table 9 **Tariffs and opportunity costs in a cost of illness study in glaucoma in Germany**

Resources	DM per unit (1997)	
	Tariff (billed quarterly by providers to the insurer)	Cost (based on time, supplies and practice overheads)
Visits to an ophthalmologist (weighted for proportion of active and retired patients)		
● First visit in quarter	19.11	34.62
● Subsequent visits in quarter	3.56	34.62
Tests performed		
● Goldman	0	13.71
● Perimetry	28.48	12.64
● Gonioscopy	9.26	4.68
● Ophthalmoscopy	0	5.20
Telephone consultation	3.56	3.68
Trabeculectomy (surgery, excluding bed-days)	149.52	377.85

Source: Kobelt et al, Graefe's Arch Clin Exp Ophth 1998, 236:811-821

the market price, in this case equivalent to the salary including employers' costs of employment. A day of sick leave, or the years of working time lost in the case of early retirement or premature death, will hence be estimated based on the average salary (if possible, age and sex adjusted). However, there is an ongoing discussion as to whether this method does not over-estimate indirect costs. In periods of high unemployment, for instance, it has been argued that productivity losses may be limited by replacing workers on early retirement after some time lag. For short term absences, production losses may be mitigated by temporarily redistributing the work of the sick worker to other employees. As a consequence, some researchers use a different method, called the "friction method", which leads to different estimates.

Since any attempt, in the short term, to compensate for lost output due to absence from work will involve some costs, for example firms maintaining spare capacity in the work force or overtime working, differences between human capital estimates and friction cost estimates will tend to be less pronounced for temporary than permanent absences. Where the results of the two methods differ substantially is in their estimates of productivity costs due to mortality and long term disability. Under the human capital approach, the cost is estimated as the gross wages that the disabled worker could otherwise have expected to earn, over the entire period of disability (or in the case of mortality, from death until the expected retirement age). In contrast, the friction cost method allows for replacement of such workers, after a period of time known as the friction period during which the labour market adjusts, from a pool of unemployed who would like to work at the going wage rate but who are unable to obtain employment. For a comparison of human capital and friction cost estimates, see Koopmanschap et al. (1995).

Guidelines for economic evaluation differ on the issue of whether indirect costs should be included, and if so under what circumstances, in an economic evaluation. Australia and the UK, for example, while allowing that indirect costs are admissible, prefer in general that evaluations should include only costs to the health care system. Canada and most of the more recent guidelines prefer the societal perspective with all costs, but demand that they be presented in a disaggregated fashion.

2.4 Cost of illness (COI) studies

Cost of illness or burden of illness studies are not concerned with a particular health care intervention but attempt to estimate the economic burden that a defined disease places upon society. As previously noted, such studies should not be categorised as economic evaluations as they do not examine outcomes. Since they do not assess the improvement in health from any specific intervention for a disease, they cannot indicate where resources should be invested to achieve most health gain. No matter how great the cost of a disease, devoting resources to it serves no purpose if there are no effective treatments. Instead, cost of illness analyses act as points of reference for economic analyses. Most studies are limited to estimating direct and indirect costs, although intangible costs are sometimes calculated. Costs can be analysed either on a prevalence basis or on an incidence basis.

2.4.1 Prevalence based studies
In prevalence based studies, all costs for a patient population in a given geographical area for a given period of time (generally one year) are estimated. Such studies are useful to health policy makers for planning and budget decisions. An example would be the amount a given country spends per year on caring for patients with Alzheimer's disease. As more people live until an advanced age, the number of patients with Alzheimer's disease will increase, and it is important to foresee and plan for the increase in costs. If analyses for several years are available, it is possible to evaluate how costs have developed and even forecast further development. An example of prevalence-based cost of illness estimates in cancer is given in Table 10. These studies will also demonstrate how the costs are distributed between direct and

Table 10 **Cost of cancer (prevalence estimates, 1990 prices)**

Country	Year	Direct costs (millions)	Indirect costs (millions)	Total costs (millions)	Direct costs as % of total health expenditure
USA	1975	$5279 23.6%	$17079 76.4%	$22358 100%	8.5%
	1985	$18104 25%	$54390 75%	$72494 100%	10.7%
Sweden	1975	1200 SEK 22%	4250 SEK 78%	5450 SEK 100%	7.4%
	1985	3300 SEK 29.5%	7900 SEK 70.5%	11200 SEK 100%	6.9%

Source: Jönsson and Karlsson (1990)

Figure 6 **Mean total costs of multiple sclerosis in the UK (1999, British pounds)**

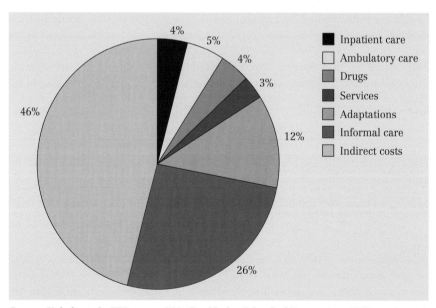

Source: Kobelt et al., EFI report 398, Stockholm School of Economics, 2000

Inpatient care	685	Adaptations	1984
Ambulatory care	869	Informal care	4373
Drugs	626	Indirect costs	7695
Services	488		

Table 11 **Direct health care costs in Sweden 1983, by main disease categories**

Disease category	Hospital (%)	Other (%)	Drugs (%)	% of total direct costs
Infective/parasitic diseases	49	41	10	1.6
Neoplasms	92	5	3	5.1
Endocrine and metabolic diseases	62	24	14	2.3
Diseases of the blood	59	33	3	0.5
Mental disorders	93	6	1	21.1
Diseases of the nervous system	59	32	9	4.2
Diseases of the circulatory system	75	15	10	12.3
Diseases of the respiratory system	51	36	13	5.0
Diseases of the digestive system	60	24	16	3.8
Diseases of the genito-urinary system	55	36	9	3.0
Complications of pregnancy/birth	71	28	1	2.7
Diseases of skin/subcutaneous tissues	28	57	15	1.7
Diseases of musculoskeletal system	54	35	11	3.9
Congenital anomalies	84	15	1	0.5
Perinatal morbidity and mortality	97	2	1	0.5
Symptoms and ill-defined conditions	39	47	14	5.1
Accidents, poisoning, violence	83	16	1	4.8
All other or unallocated				21.9
Total				100%

Source: Lindgren, 1990

indirect costs within a disease and where the major expenses occur, as shown in Figure 6. When analyses are available for all major disease areas in a country, national policy makers gain insight into where the majority of the country's health care resources are spent, as shown for Sweden in Table 11. If studies are performed in several countries, using the same methodology, treatment strategies in different countries can be compared, as shown in the following Study Example 1.

Study Example 1 – *Prevalence-based COI – Multiple Sclerosis in three countries*

Multiple Sclerosis (MS) is an autoimmune disease that affects young adults and leads rapidly to severe physical disability. The recent introduction of several expensive new treatments, aimed at slowing progression of MS, has focused attention on current and potential future expenditures, and a number of

Table 12 Cost per patient and total annual costs of MS in three countries

	Sweden	*UK*	*Germany*
Estimated prevalence	11,000	88,000	120,000
Cost per MS case	45,000 €	28,000 €	33,500 €
Total estimated costs	0.5 billion €	2.2 billion €	4.0 billion €
Cost per inhabitant	56 €	36 €	50 €

studies have been performed. They generally found that indirect costs constitute the vast majority of the costs (70-80%). However, most of the studies were top down (see section 2.4.3) or involved very small samples, hence costs outside the health care system were not captured. Also, limited information on how costs and quality of life evolve with advancing disease was available. Both these questions are important in a setting where treatments aim to delay progression to severe disability.

A recent observational study in three countries collected information about resource use, quality of life and disease parameters directly from around 1800 patients using a detailed questionnaire. The sample was population based insofar as it included either all patients in a geographic area (the region of Stockholm for Sweden), all patients on file in specialized MS centres (in the UK) or those who had been in contact with such centres during the past two years (in Germany). Hence, it was possible to extrapolate from the cost per case to the total annual costs in each country, as shown in Table 12. As expected, when all costs are included, total expenditures were much higher than previously estimated, and the proportion of costs represented by indirect costs is considerably lower than previously estimated (Figure 7). It is also interesting to note the marked differences in direct spending in the three countries, while indirect costs are similar. The explanation for this is that the effect of the disease on patients' ability to work is the same in all countries and there is little influence of the system, while health care and social support can be organized in very different ways. Most importantly, however, costs and quality of life were strongly correlated with the severity of the disease, as shown in Figures 8 and 9.

Several issues need to be considered when collecting information directly from patients. The recall of events may not be perfect and patients may overstate or understate resource use. Also, patients may find it difficult to distinguish between costs related directly to the disease and other resource use. The latter is a problem in many diseases where, for instance, general medical practitioners (general, primary care physicians) are involved in providing care. However, in MS it was not considered a problem, as patients are generally young and hence co-morbidity is limited. The accuracy of recall is a difficulty in all areas and, in general, the recommended period for data

Figure 7 **Distribution of mean costs per patient by category of cost**

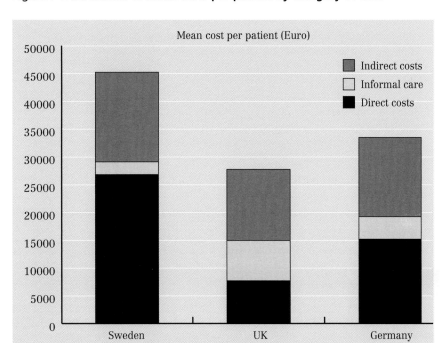

collection is one to three months. In this study, patients were asked for consumption in the last three months, except for hospitalization and large investments where 12 months was considered feasible. Clearly, however, some control mechanism is required, so medical charts for a sub-sample of patients were reviewed to compare their answers with the hospital records. From this it appeared that there was no recall bias, as for instance in Germany the mean number of inpatient days in the charts and in the questionnaires for a sample of 105 patients who were hospitalised were virtually the same (means of 26.90 and 27.15 days with similar ranges).

References

Henriksson F, Fredrikson S, Masterman T, Jönsson B (2001). Costs, quality of life and disease severity in multiple sclerosis. A cross-sectional study in Sweden. *European Journal of Neurology* 8:27-35.

Kobelt G, Lindgren P, Smala A, Jönsson B, and the German Cost of MS Group (2001). Costs and quality of life in multiple sclerosis. An observational study in Germany. *HEPAC* 2(2):60-68.

Kobelt G, Lindgren P, Parkin D, Francis D, Johnson M, Bates D (2000). Costs and quality of life in multiple sclerosis. A cross-sectional observational study in the United Kingdom. Stockholm: Stockholm School of Economics, EFI Research Report No 398.

Figure 8 Mean annual cost per patient by severity of the disease

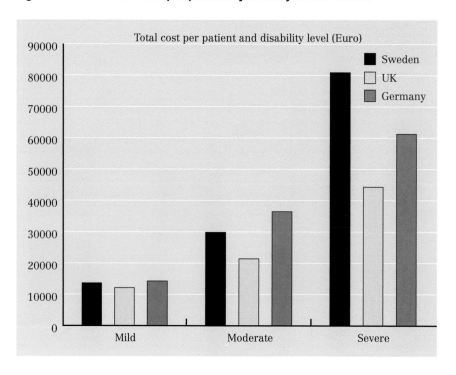

Figure 9 Mean utility (quality of life) by severity of the disease

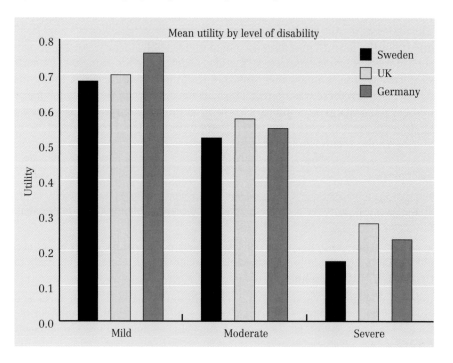

2.4.2 Incidence based studies

In *incidence based studies*, life-time costs for a patient with the disease, from diagnosis to cure or, in chronic diseases, to death, are estimated. These studies are more useful when estimating the effect of a treatment on future costs. Using the example of Alzheimer's disease again, such studies are useful to see what type of costs a treatment that prevents the loss of mental faculties could potentially avoid, for example nursing care. Table 13 gives an example of a study in leukaemia. Incidence based studies are difficult to perform in chronic diseases that span decades, and are therefore often limited to costs per case over a given number of years, in order to identify what treatment strategies prevail and what drives the costs (see Study Example 2).

2.4.3 Costing methods

The data for cost of illness studies can be identified from different sources such as national health care statistics, patient registries, cohort studies, insurance databases, patient charts or from patients themselves. Dependent on the availability of data in official statistics and national databases, and the level of detail that is required to answer the study question, studies are performed "top-down" or "bottom-up".

In *top-down studies*, statistical databases and registries are used to estimate the costs for a given prevalence sample. The problem with this approach is that in most countries, some costs for diseases such as Alzheimer's disease and the majority of costs for multiple sclerosis are usually not found in these registries and total costs will therefore be underestimated.

In *bottom-up studies*, costs are collected directly from a patient sample, either retrospectively by using patient charts and questionnaires, or prospectively by following the sample for a given time. The difficulty with this approach is to ensure that the sample is unbiased and representative of the overall patient population.

Table 13 **Cost of acute myeloid leukaemia in Sweden (incidence estimate, 1980)**

Activity	Costs (SEK)	Percent
Hospital/hotel/physician	72200	70
Blood products	10600	10
Laboratory tests	3100	3
Drugs – cytotoxic drugs	5700	6
Drugs – antibiotics	4500	4
Cultures	2100	2
Other activities	4900	5
Total treatment cost	103100	100

Source: Jönsson and Karlsson, 1990

Table 14 **Differences in costs between top-down and bottom-up cost of illness studies in multiple sclerosis in Sweden (prevalence 11,000)**

	Top-down 1991*	Top-down 1994*	Bottom-up 1999**
	Million SEK	Million SEK	Million SEK
Direct costs	428	370	2897
Hospital	413	354	649
Ambulatory care	13	13	364
Drugs	2	3	164
Other			1720
Indirect costs	1260	1506	1602
Sickness absence	77	183	87
Early retirement	1008	1183	1515
Mortality	175	140	–
Total costs	1688	1876	4499

* Henriksson and Jönsson, 1998 PharmacoEconomics 13,597-606
** Henriksson et al., 2001 Eur.J.Neurolog

Tables 14 and 15 illustrate the differences between top-down and bottom-up cost of illness studies performed in Sweden and Germany.

Table 15 **Differences in costs between top-down and bottom-up cost of illness studies in multiple sclerosis in Germany (prevalence 120,000)**

	Top-down 1997/8*	Bottom-up 1999**	Bottom-up 1999**
	Public payer perspective	Public payer perspective	Societal perspective
Direct costs	1031	2047	4525
Inpatient care	353	750	804
Ambulatory care	437	477	556
Drugs (interferons)	143	344	186
Drugs (other)	75	154	365
Services, adaptations	23	322	1664
Informal care	–	–	950
Indirect costs	421	930	3340
Sickness absence	133	50	296
Early retirement	288	880	3044
Total costs	1452	2977	7865

* Upmeier and Miltenburger, ISTAHC 2000
** Kobelt et al., HEPAC 2001:60-68

Study Example 2 – *Incidence based cost of illness – Glaucoma in nine countries*

Glaucoma affects mainly the elderly and is characterized by a gradual restriction of the visual field due to damage to the optic nerve with the potential to lead to blindness. The causes and progression of the disease are not fully understood, but elevated intra-ocular pressure (IOP) is considered the major risk factor and is hence the main target of all treatments (pharmacological and surgical). In such a case, a prevalence-based study to investigate annual spending on the disease would be useful to forecast the increase in expenditures as the population ages. However, if it is intended that the study should form the basis for a cost-effectiveness analysis of a new treatment, it is important to investigate how treatment patterns and costs develop over time for individual patients or patient groups. Thus a longitudinal study of patients newly diagnosed will be more useful, even if it does not cover the time span from diagnosis to death.

This study was performed as a retrospective chart review in nine countries, covering the first two years of treatment after diagnosis, and the main purpose was to establish a baseline of current clinical practice to estimate the impact of the introduction of a new therapy. Specifically, the analysis included patients who, at a point in time, would qualify for the new therapy. The study investigated the time to failure of first-line therapy and the preferred treatment strategies thereafter, as well as the major drivers of costs and differences between countries.

Study sites were selected based on the organisation of ophthalmic care in each country and patient files were searched from December 1994 backwards, including all patients with complete two-year data until a sample of at least 200 was reached. Medical data were limited to detailed diagnosis and development of IOP over two years, but all resource utilisation related to glaucoma was included. Resources were valued at their opportunity cost, but the data were limited to direct health care consumption.

The study found that medical parameters were surprisingly similar. For instance, in all nine countries, the mean post-treatment IOP was 18 mmHg, despite the fact that the mean at diagnosis varied from 31 mmHg (Germany and Sweden) to 24 mmHg (France). However, the treatment paths to reach this target level were vastly different, as can be seen in Figure 10. As a consequence, costs were very different as well, although it should be borne in mind that the comparison has to be interpreted with care, due to the differences in prices and health care organisation mentioned earlier (Figure 11).

Multiple regression analysis identified IOP and change of IOP with treatment as the main cost driver, i.e. overall costs increased by approximately 4% for each mmHg higher IOP at diagnosis, and they decreased by around 3% for each mmHg decrease in IOP with treatment in all countries in the analysis. This was due to more intensive management when IOP is higher, and more treatment changes when treatment is not fully satisfactory. Thus, in all countries, costs increased with each treatment change, as illustrated in Table 16 for the UK and US.

Figure 10 **Differences in the choice of treatment and patient management in different countries**

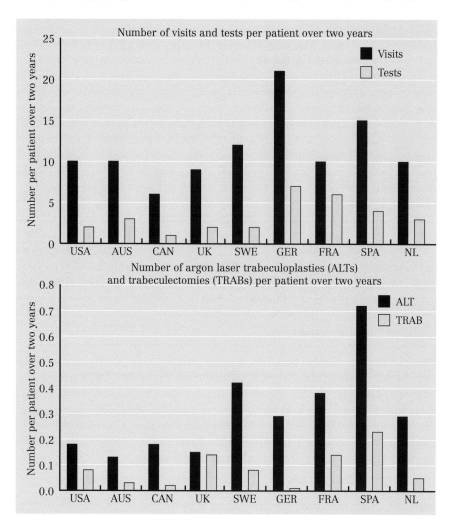

The treatment sequences and cost drivers thus identified in this study served as basis for a model to estimate the impact of a new drug (see Study Example 4).

One issue that has been discussed regarding this study is retrospective data collection. Analysing clinical records retrospectively has obvious limitations, such as the lack of control as to how the data were obtained and, more importantly, missing data. Thus, prospective data collection may be preferable to ensure that all information is available and in an appropriate format. However, for resource utilisation, a retrospective design has certain advantages: the data have not been influenced by any protocol or study design and thus represent true clinical practice, and the study can be carried out in a relatively short timeframe.

Figure 11 Differences in costs depending on the use of estimates based on insurance tariffs or full opportunity costs

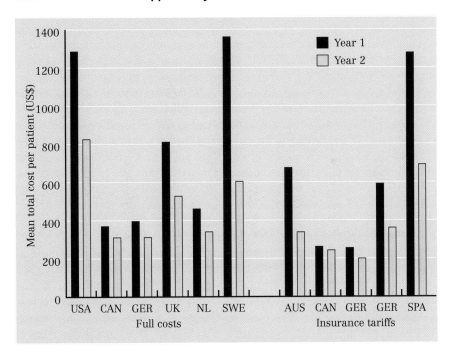

Table 16 Mean two-year costs per patient by the number of therapy changes

Number of changes	UK		USA	
	% of patients	Costs (£)	% of patients	Costs (US$)
0	73	372	53	1424
1	15	1346	18	2121
2	8	2788	13	2950
3 or more	4	2834	16	4458

References

Jönsson B, Krieglstein G (eds.) (1998). Primary-open angle glaucoma. Differences in international treatment patterns and cost. Isis Medical Media, Oxford, UK.

Kobelt G, Gerdtham UG, Alm A (1998). Costs of treating primary open angle glaucoma. Journal of Glaucoma, 7, 95-104.

Kobelt G, Jönsson L, Gerdtham U, Krieglstein GK (1998). Direct costs of glaucoma management following initiation of medical therapy. Graefe's Archives for Clinical and Experimental Ophthalmology 236: 811-821.

Kobelt G, Jönsson L (1999). Modelling cost of patient management with new topical treatments for glaucoma. Results for France and the UK. International Journal of Technology Assessment in Health Care 15:1, 207-219.

2.5 Consequences (outcome measurement)

In clinical trials, as in clinical practice, several measures can be used to express the outcome in a disease, as they may address different treatment effects that are of importance to clinical management. In economic evaluation, on the other hand, outcomes should ideally be expressed using one effectiveness measure that is easy to understand and to relate to the disease, and that ultimately can be compared to outcomes across diseases. The measure should also express the overall and final outcomes rather than intermediate ones. In acute and curable diseases, such as infections, it is rather easy to define the final outcome in a dichotomous way as "cure" or "no cure", and the economic evaluation will then estimate and compare the costs of achieving the cure with different treatment strategies. In chronic diseases, particularly in chronic progressive diseases, defining an overall final outcome is more difficult and the efficacy of treatments is generally assessed based on intermediate endpoints, such as relapse rate.

2.5.1 Physiological measures and clinical events

Physiological measures such as mmHg in hypertension, mMol cholesterol in hyperlipidaemia, and bone mineral density in osteoporosis, are routinely used in clinical management as outcome measures, as they are linked to clinical events such as stroke, myocardial infarction and fractures. In these cases, economic evaluation can then estimate the value of avoiding (or postponing) an event, provided that epidemiological data linking the surrogate measure to the undesirable event are available. If it is possible to derive a risk function for the annual risk of, for example, a hip fracture at a given level of bone mineral density and at a given age, or of a myocardial infarction at a given level of cholesterol, controlled for age and gender, then the cost-effectiveness of treatment today with the aim to avoid an event that occurs in the future can be estimated. Figure 12 illustrates this concept.

Using epidemiological data to derive a risk function for the annual risk of a serious clinical event at given levels of the surrogate measure and under different conditions (age, sex, risk factors), it is possible to link short term intermediate endpoints with final outcomes, and to calculate the cost-effectiveness of treatments that aim to reduce the risk.

However, the true objective of preventing serious clinical events is to avoid the consequences of the event rather than the event itself, often a risk of death or serious disability. Economic evaluation will preferably attempt to capture the consequences of avoiding the event as the outcome of treatment rather than the avoidance of the event, by estimating changes in survival and quality of life.

2.5.2 Survival

Survival can be measured in different ways, for example: the proportion of patients alive in each group at the end of a clinical trial or conversely as the number of deaths avoided, the number of patients alive after five years, or overall survival. In prevention, for example in cardiology, not only are the total

Figure 12 **Extrapolating from intermediate to final outcome**

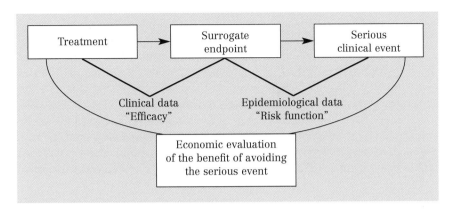

number of deaths or the number of cardiovascular deaths recorded but also the number of non-fatal myocardial infarctions. In economic evaluation, survival is generally measured as the number of years of life, representing an area under the survival curve that can be related both to costs and to quality of life. However, clinical trials are seldom long enough to provide the data necessary to estimate directly the number of life years saved (LYS) by one treatment compared to another and epidemiological data are again required to extrapolate from the short-term perspective of lives saved to the long-term perspective of life expectancy. Figure 13 illustrates the concept of LYS and shows that the effects of a treatment achieved within trials carry over to the period after the trial.

A difference in the number of patients alive at the end of a clinical trial will have an effect during the years after the trial. For instance, if we assume that 5% of patients surviving at year five die every year after the trial in both groups, everybody will be dead after 20 years. Mean and median survival will be 10 years. If we further assume that survival at the end of the trial was 80% in the control group and 90% in the intervention group, the gain in life expectancy in the intervention group will be 0.25 years during the trial [({5*0.9}+{5*0.1/2}) – ({5*0.8}+{5*0.2/2})] and one year after the trial [(20*0.9/2)-(20*0.8/2)]. The life expectancy at the start of the trial will be 12.5 years in the control group and 13.75 years in the intervention group, and the majority of the difference is achieved after the clinical trial. The area between the two curves in the figure above represents the difference in life-expectancy in the two groups.

2.5.3 Quality-adjusted survival

Outcome measurement in chronic or progressive diseases (such as Alzheimer's disease, Parkinson's disease, multiple sclerosis, rheumatoid arthritis) is more difficult, as there are often no distinct events which have an impact on survival. Rather, patients experience a continuous decrease in physical and/or mental abilities over a long time. Often such diseases affect

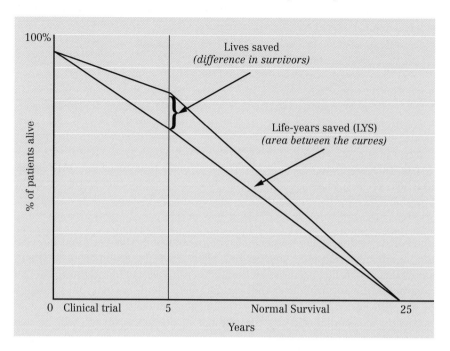

several functions and produce a number of different symptoms, leading researchers to seek an outcome that encompasses all effects. The most frequently used such measure in economic evaluation is the quality-adjusted life year (QALY), which captures the overall effect of a disease on quality of life over a given time, and combines quantity and quality of life gained with a treatment. QALYs can be compared across diseases and, as a consequence, are the preferred outcome measure by government bodies or other authorities that require economic evaluation prior to recommending a treatment be provided from public funds, such as the National Institute for Clinical Excellence (NICE) in the UK.

QALYs are calculated by adjusting time (years of life) with an index that expresses global quality of life (utility) on a scale between 0 (death) and 1 (full health). Utility can be measured using techniques from decision analysis that are explained later in this book. For example, if being blind has a utility of 0.4, spending 10 years as a blind person would give four QALYs, which is equivalent to spending four years in full health. Thus, using QALYs as an outcome, treatments in different diseases can be compared. Treatments that prolong life can be assessed in the same way as ones that improve quality of life. Figure 14 illustrates this concept.

In order to compare QALYs from different studies, they need to be measured using the same methods. This is not always done in practice, and their use has therefore been met with some scepticism. There is also an ethical element –

the implicit assumption underlying the use of QALYs is that the health care system should maximise QALYs by choosing the treatments with the lowest cost per QALY. Without attempting to do justice to the vast literature on QALYs, it is possible here to give a flavour of the criticisms made against the QALY. Some of these centre around the idea that QALYs do not reflect people's preferences towards survival and quality of life. Taking the example used in the previous paragraph where blindness was valued at 0.4, QALY calculations give 4 QALYs where this health state is experienced over 10 years, 8 QALYs for a twenty year duration and so on. However, it is possible either that some health states become less tolerable over time or that they appear less severe because people adjust to their condition. Twenty years in a state of blindness may therefore seem worth less than twice or more than twice the QALY value attached to ten years in this state. For some states of health initially considered preferable to immediate death (i.e. with a positive score), there may be a survival duration at which any further survival seems less preferred than immediate death, so that a shorter period of survival in those states is preferable to a longer period; Stalmeier et al. (2001) provide some evidence on this. From an equity perspective, it is sometimes argued that QALYs discriminate against certain groups, e.g. the elderly, as the potential number of life years that can be saved by treating an 80-year old patient is less than when treating a 40-year old. Whereas it is normally assumed that a QALY is of equal value no matter who benefits, this may not accord with the preferences of the population. In general, society may choose to give priority to certain groups and want to ensure that these patients have access to treatments even though the cost per QALY may be high. However, while the QALY is certainly not a perfect measure, its use is currently widespread, as it is the best measure available for making comparisons across disease areas.

2.5.4 Monetary outcomes

In cost-benefit analysis, the outcome of a treatment is expressed as the willingness of individuals or society to pay for it. Monetary outcomes have met with some scepticism in the medical field, mostly due to the reluctance mentioned above to define a threshold value that society should be paying for

Figure 14 **The concept of Quality-Adjusted Life Years**

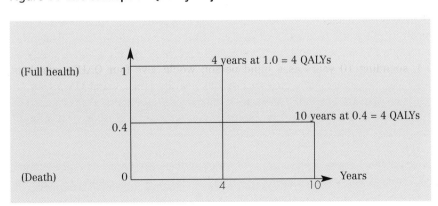

a given outcome, e.g. a life year or a QALY. Also, the techniques for measuring willingness to pay have not been as well tested within the health care environment as techniques for measuring utilities.

2.5.5 Patient reported outcomes

The interest in measuring patient reported outcome, i.e. patients' subjective well-being, has increased in recent years. There are several explanations for this, one of them being the increasing number of people with chronic diseases, where one of the major impacts of the disease will be on patients' quality of life and where the objective of treatment is to improve patients' physical, mental and social functioning. The classical clinical measures are often inadequate to describe and evaluate this effect, and a number of instruments to measure health-related quality of life have been developed, both generic and disease-specific. These instruments are designed to elicit patients' subjective evaluations of the effects of a disease or a treatment and have become an important tool for the assessment of outcomes. However, for the purposes of cost-utility analysis, these measurements can only be used if they are expressed as an index or a weight, with clearly defined anchors between the worst and the best health states.

Health-related quality of life has been defined by the WHO as a combination of physical, mental and social well-being, not merely the absence of disease, and, in general, measurements are carried out along these three dimensions. Table 17 lists some of the concepts measured.

Table 17 **Dimensions in patient reported outcomes**

	Dimension	*Includes*
Physical dimension	Physical function	Mobility, activities of daily living, etc.
	Symptoms	Pain, fatigue, nausea, etc.
	Role activities	Work, household tasks
Mental dimension	Psychological well-being	Happiness, depression, anxiety, etc.
	Personal constructs	Spirituality, life satisfaction
	Cognitive functioning	Memory, concentration, etc.
Social dimension	Social functioning	Family life, social contact, friendship
	Social well-being	Stigma, degree of isolation
Overall	Global judgement of health	Overall rating of current health
	Satisfaction with care	Satisfaction with treatment

Instruments to measure patient reported outcomes fall into three basic categories that are used in different circumstances and for different purposes:
– generic measures
– disease-specific measures
– preference-based measures (utility measures).

Generic measures were developed to assess health status across all diseases and of relevance to all health problems. They have the advantage that the impact of a treatment in one disease can be compared with that of treatment for other diseases. A potential drawback of generic instruments is that they may fail to capture small effects specific to a disease. To address this limitation, disease-specific instruments have been developed for many diseases. They measure the distinctive aspects of diseases missed by generic measures, and provide valuable information in clinical trials, assessment of specific needs or patient monitoring. However, they are not useful for comparison between diseases and can hence not be used in decisions relating to resource allocation across therapy areas. The third category of instruments, the utility measures, are of particular interest to economists because they yield a set of weights on which QALY calculations can be based. Some generic instruments will yield an overall quality of life score as an index and can therefore be treated as utility measures suitable for generating QALYs. The EuroQol EQ-5D is often used in this way. Another frequently used generic measure, the SF-36, does not, in contrast, produce an overall index and cannot therefore be applied to the calculation of QALYs.

All outcome instruments must stand up to scrutiny for reliability, reproducibility, validity, feasibility and sensitivity to change and can be assessed against these criteria using psychometric techniques. Table 18 presents some of the better known instruments.

Table 18 **Established health related quality of life instruments**

Type of instrument	*Example instruments*
General health profiles	Short Form 36 (SF-36), Nottingham Health Profile (NHP), Sickness Impact Profile (SIP), General Well-Being Scale
General health indices	Index of Well-Being, EuroQol EQ-5D, Health Utilities Index (HUI)
Disease specific scales	Arthritis Impact Measurement Scale (AIMS), Minnesota Living with Heart Disease Scale, Multiple Sclerosis Quality of Life Inventory (MSQLI), Beck Depression Inventory (BDI)

The development of a quality of life instrument is a cumbersome process that can span several years. The MOS Short Form 36 (SF-36), for example, was developed over a period of 10 years, using questionnaires and data from the Rand Medical Outcomes Study in the US and translated, adapted and validated across 10-15 countries over a further 4-5 years. Acceptability of a new instrument will depend on its use in several different investigations, thus adding a further delay to its widespread use. Therefore, development of new disease-specific instruments should only be undertaken when an adequate instrument is not available and this lack cannot be overcome, for instance, by using several existing instruments which together address the concepts required.

3 Analytical Approaches to Economic Evaluation

The most straightforward way to estimate costs and consequences is to use resource utilisation and efficacy data from a randomized clinical trial. This approach retains the high internal validity of the trial, ensures that both the costs and the effects are measured within the same setting, and allows variability in cost and effect estimates to be explored using confidence intervals for the incremental cost-effectiveness ratio (ICER). Conventional statistical methods can be applied to the analysis of uncertainty around the ICER but analysts are also exploring the use of Bayesian approaches to this problem within the clinical trial setting; the interested reader is referred to Briggs (2001) and Al and van Hout (2000) for examples of their application.

However, there are several reasons why this approach may not be suitable in practice. First, in many diseases it is impossible to fund a study enrolling enough subjects for a long enough time period to collect the necessary data. Second, the special circumstances of clinical studies will influence patient management and some costs will be entirely protocol-driven, preventing a relevant comparison to clinical practice. Third, many studies enrol patients in a large number of countries and the individual national groups are therefore generally too small to assess country-specific costs as would be needed for an economic evaluation. Although the way to handle this latter problem in the past has been to use the quantities of resources from the entire trial and apply country-specific unit costs to them, this may not be a fully satisfactory solution as patient management between countries may be different. Willke et al. (1998) propose a method for adapting the results of a multinational clinical trial to the circumstances of individual countries, but recognize the method's limitations, one of which is that it cannot address the issue of deviations from usual care introduced by the study protocol. Additionally, trials are powered for the full sample and individual country samples may therefore be too small. However, the method provides additional information on the variation between countries. Lastly, participation in a clinical trial will tend to be restricted to a narrowly defined group of patients as specified in the protocol and the difference between, for example, a treatment and placebo may therefore not be entirely representative of the broader population of patients with the condition being treated.

These characteristics may mean that the efficacy results from trials are of limited generalizability beyond the trial to effectiveness in routine clinical practice. Moreover, there will be situations in which there is no experimental data on costs and effects relating to the question which the decision maker wants to address, perhaps because trials have been based on placebo controls rather than a comparator relevant to treatment decisions made in practice. Thus, modelling costs and effects by synthesising data from different sources (epidemiological, clinical, economic) becomes necessary.

Within models, it is possible to combine different data sets, extrapolate to a longer time frame than clinical trials, test different assumptions about risk, effectiveness, costs, etc. Economic evaluations generally use two types of models:

- For cost-effectiveness analysis in diseases with distinct events that occur with a given probability, either by decision or by chance, within a relatively limited time frame, decision tree models are used.

- For analyses in diseases with an ongoing risk, over a long time frame, Markov models are more appropriate.

3.1 Decision analysis

Decision analysis was developed as a discipline for examining choices under uncertainty and has long been applied to clinical decision making. It enables complex problems and processes to be broken down into component parts, each of which can be analysed individually in detail before they are recombined in a logical, quantitative and temporal way to indicate the best course of action. Analyses can be depicted as a decision tree that incorporates strategic choices, probabilities of subsequent events and final outcomes. An example is given in Figure 15.

Several steps are required to construct a clinical decision tree: clear definition of the problem; description of successful or unsuccessful outcomes; definition of alternative patient management strategies and their consequences; estimation of the probabilities; and a time frame.

Decision trees are usually based on data from clinical trials and other sources of empirical evidence, such as systematic reviews and meta-analyses. For the economic evaluation, the expected cost for each strategy is calculated by multiplying the cost for each branch by the overall probability of that branch occurring. The different treatment strategies can then be compared in terms of their different expected costs and outcomes.

3.2 Markov chain analysis

Sometimes, decision trees will not be the best way to describe disease effects and interventions. This is particularly the case in chronic diseases where the risk of, for example, progression of a disease, may be continuously changing over time and where the timing of events is important. For such problems, a Markov model will be more appropriate. Figure 16 illustrates the structure of Markov models.

For Markov models, it is assumed that all patients can be classified into a finite number of states, so called Markov states. States are generally defined by

Figure 15 **Decision trees**

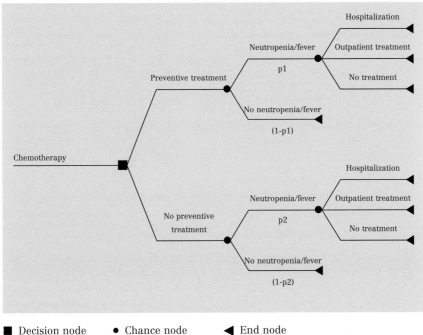

■ Decision node   ● Chance node   ◄ End node

Notes:

In this example of a decision tree, a decision is made to give or not give a treatment that reduces the risk of chemotherapy-induced neutropenia (decision node). In both cases, patients can have neutropenia, but the probability (chance node) in the intervention group (p1) is lower than in the no treatment group (p2). Consequently, costs of treating neutropenia are lower in the intervention group, as fewer patients experience it, assuming that it is treated in the same way in both groups. Expected costs and expected outcomes for each strategy will be estimated by "folding back the tree".

Using the decision tree model above, if we assume that the preventive treatment costs € 1000, that the average proportion of patients experiencing neutropenia without prevention is 40%, that treatment reduces this risk by 25%, and that the average cost of treating a neutropenic event is € 3000, the average cost per patient in the prevention arm would be € 1900 (€ (1000 + 0.3 x 3000)) and in the no prevention arm € 1200 (€ 3000 x 0.4).

The cost-effectiveness of preventive treatment will be estimated by comparing the two strategies. In this example, the incremental cost per neutropenic event avoided would be € 7000 (€700/0.1). In other words, preventive treatment would reduce the absolute proportion of patients with neutropenic events by 10%, thereby saving € 300 (€ 3000 x 0.1) and leaving an incremental cost for the preventive treatment of € 700 (€ 1000 - € 300).

disease parameters, such as severity of a disease, that are meaningful to patients and clinicians, but other definitions exist as well. Development of a disease and the effect of treatment are represented as transitions from one state to another. Disease progression will be represented by transitions to more severe states, while the treatment effect will either reverse or slow this

Figure 16 **Markov models**

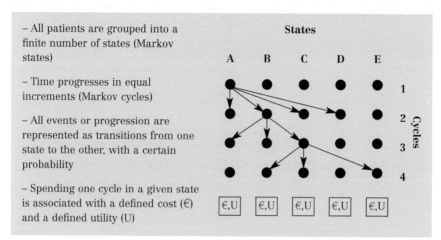

- All patients are grouped into a finite number of states (Markov states)

- Time progresses in equal increments (Markov cycles)

- All events or progression are represented as transitions from one state to the other, with a certain probability

- Spending one cycle in a given state is associated with a defined cost (€) and a defined utility (U)

Notes:

Markov models illustrate the disease process by distributing patients across a finite number of distinct and mutually exclusive disease states at baseline and then following the development of the cohort during a defined time (number of cycles).

For instance, states could be defined by levels of disability, with state A above being "no disability", B "mild disability", C "moderate disability", D "severe disability" and E "death" (absorbing state). All Markov models have a state that patients cannot leave, usually death, in order to perform survival analyses. However, often there is not enough detailed information to perform lifetime analyses, and the duration of the model, i.e. the number of cycles as well as their length, is chosen depending on the disease and the epidemiological and clinical data that are available.

Costs and utilities (health status) for these states are assumed to depend on the state only and are therefore the same for all cycles. In such a framework, more severe states are generally associated with higher disease costs and a lower quality of life. Thus, if patients spend more time in the benign states of "no disability" or "mild disability", costs within a given time frame will be reduced while quality of life will be improved.

The transitions between states, i.e. the probability at each cycle of deterioration (e.g. from moderate to severe disability) or of improvement (e.g. from moderate to mild disability) are calculated from epidemiological or clinical data.

The model will then calculate the average cumulative costs and effects, e.g. the number of QALYs, over a defined time for an untreated and a treated cohort, and compare the groups to estimate the incremental cost (treatment costs minus cost reductions due to treatment) per QALY gained with the treatment compared with no treatment.

progression. The differences or cut-off points between the states must therefore also represent clinically meaningful differences.

The time period covered by a model is divided into equal increments, referred to as Markov cycles. The length of the cycle is chosen to represent a clinically meaningful time interval. For instance, weekly cycles in a model to calculate the effectiveness of a treatment to avoid hip fractures would clearly be too short, while yearly cycles for a treatment of infections would be too long. During each cycle a patient may make a transition from one state to another, or remain in the current state. No distinction is made between the different patients within each state.

The probabilities of making a transition from one state to another during a cycle (transition probabilities) are generally calculated from epidemiological data or clinical trials. The Markov process is completely defined by the cohort distribution among the states at the start and the probabilities for the individual transitions allowed during the subsequent cycles. In order for a Markov process to terminate, it must have at least one state that the patient cannot leave. Such states are called absorbing states because, after a sufficient number of cycles, the entire cohort will have been absorbed by those states. In medical examples, death is by far the most common absorbing state.

Each state is assigned a utility and a cost, and cumulative utilities and costs for a given cohort are calculated at the end of the Markov process.

Markov processes are commonly represented as so-called state transition diagrams, as shown schematically in Figure 17. A newer representation of Markov models, the Markov cycle tree, shown in Figure 18, seems, however, a more convenient way of illustrating these models.

Figure 17

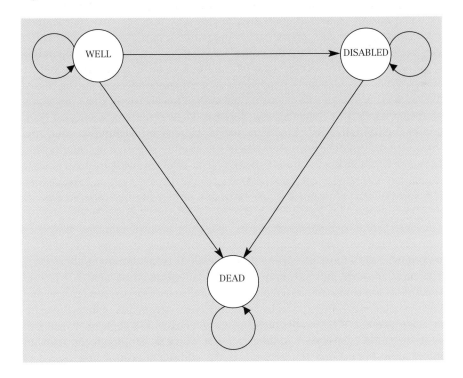

Figure 18

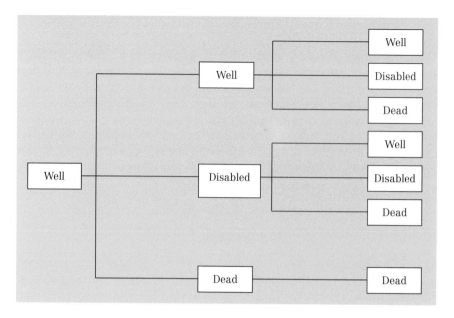

3.3 Calculation of cost-effectiveness ratios

The second stage of economic evaluation is to compare the expected costs and expected effects of the different treatments. The average cost-effectiveness ratio illustrates the cost, on average, of reaching a particular outcome with a given treatment, for instance the cost to save one life year (as illustrated in Box 5), usually compared with a hypothetical scenario involving no costs and no effects. While this may be of importance to get a general feeling for the cost of a treatment, it provides no relevant information for decisions about allocation of resources. If, for instance, the decision is to replace a treatment with another more effective, but also more expensive, treatment, then the important information is an estimate of the additional resources that have to be spent to obtain the additional benefit. The relevant measure in economic evaluation is therefore the *incremental cost-effectiveness ratio (ICER)*, which indicates the cost of producing one extra unit of benefit (illustrated in Box 5).

The incremental cost-effectiveness ratio is calculated by dividing the difference in costs between two treatments by the difference in their effects. If a treatment is both more effective and less costly, it is the dominant alternative. The most frequent mistake in published cost-effectiveness analyses is that treatments are compared based on their average cost-effectiveness ratios, and these studies therefore provide incomplete or erroneous information for decision-making. Where a decision maker is faced with a choice between two or more mutually exclusive options none of which is dominant, the relevant information for making the decision is the additional cost of one course of

Box 5 **Illustration of cost-effectiveness analysis**

Treatment A is the standard treatment, and treatment B is a new therapy.
Treatment A reduces 1-year mortality from 25% to 15% at a cost of €1,500.
Treatment B reduces 1-year mortality from 25% to 10% at a cost of €2,000.

Treatment A will thus save 10 life years per 100 patients and B will save 15
life years per 100 patients.

Average cost-effectiveness ratios:
A: €15,000 per life year saved (€1,500 / 0.10)
B: €13,333 per life year saved (€2,000 / 0.15)

Incremental cost-effectiveness ratio (ICER) of B compared to A:
€10,000 per additional life year saved ({2,000-1,500} / {0.15-0.10})

action relative to its additional benefits compared with the alternative. In other
words, how much additional cost must be incurred to achieve an extra unit of
health gain? The decision maker can then decide whether or not to choose the
more costly option based on a consideration of whether the extra cost is
justified by the additional benefit obtained.

Study Example 3 – *Treatment of onychomycosis*

Several treatments exist to treat fungal infections of toenails and fingernails
(onychomycoses). For toenail infections oral drugs are preferred, as topical
preparations have been shown to be of limited effectiveness. The cost-effectiveness
of four oral medicines for the treatment of onychomycosis was analysed in 12
European countries and Canada (Arikian et al., 1994). As an example, the analysis
for treatments of infection of toenails in Austria is summarised here, from the
perspective of the payer, i.e. the national health insurance fund.

The medicines compared were griseofulvin (GRI), itraconazole (ITR),
ketoconazole (KET) and terbinafine (TER). Treatment modalities with these
drugs as primary therapy were established in each country with a group of
dermatologists. The incidence of adverse effects for each drug was established
with a meta-analysis of published data and their treatment discussed with
practitioners. The cost of one course of therapy was then calculated. The
results are set out in Table 19.

A clinical decision tree for patient management over a two-year time-frame
was elaborated with the teams of dermatologists in the different countries.
Clinical outcomes were established through a thorough meta-analysis of
published clinical data and probabilities for success, failure and relapse
incorporated into the decision tree which is shown in Figure 19.

Table 19 **Treatment of fungal infection of toenails with four oral drugs: cost of one course of therapy in Austria (figures in Austrian Schillings)**

Cost item	GRI	ITR	KET	TER
Drug acquisition	3990	12240	6240	9408
Medical consultation	1100	440	880	440
Lab tests required	9466	2641	9466	2641
Treatment of side effects	10	34	694	4
Total costs	14566	15355	17280	12493

Source: Adapted from Arikian et al. (1994)

Costs for each activity in the tree were established in each country and multiplied by the probabilities in each branch to calculate the average cost per treated patient for each of the drugs. Table 20 shows the calculation for all four comparators in Austria.

In the study, the effectiveness measure was defined as "disease-free days" and the average cost-effectiveness for all comparators was calculated. However, no

Figure 19 **Clinical decision tree for treating fungal infection of the toenail (two years)**

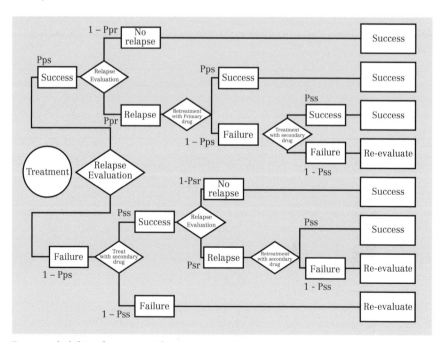

Pps = probability of success with primary treatment
Pss = probability of success with secondary treatment
Ppr = probability of relapse with primary treatment
Psr = probability of relapse with secondary treatment

Table 20 **Average cost per treated patient over two years (figures in Austrian Schillings)**

Decision branch	*GRI*	*ITR*	*KET*	*TER*
Branch 1	1529	7701	4371	9136
Branch 2	1835	5127	4822	1162
Branch 3	228	627	571	143
Branch 4	63	174	158	65
Branch 5	16326	6374	12890	3031
Branch 6	1518	587	1164	1565
Branch 7	169	65	129	174
Branch 8	4844	1892	3825	1892
Total	26512	22547	27930	17167

incremental analysis was performed, as the least costly alternative (terbinafine) was also the most effective, i.e. it was dominant. This can easily be seen in the proportions of patients achieving cure and experiencing a re-infection after one full course of therapy (see Figure 20), where terbinafine has by far the highest cure and lowest reinfection rate. Thus, in this particular case, cost-consequence analysis was all that was needed and the analysis could have stopped there.

Figure 20 **Effectiveness of four treatments for onychomycosis (proportion of patients achieving cure and experiencing re-infection after 1 course of treatment)**

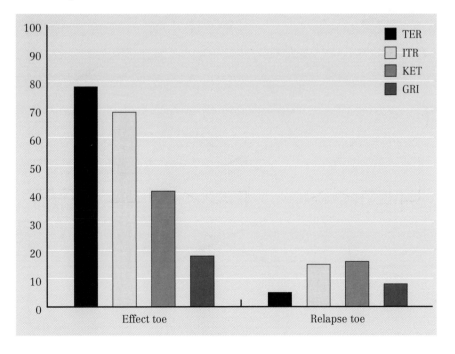

Reference

Arikian S, Einarson T, Kobelt-Nguyen G, Schubert F (1994). A multinational pharmacoeconomic analysis of oral therapies for onychomycosis. British Journal of Dermatology 130 (Suppl43):35-44.

Study Example 4 – *Treatment of glaucoma*

Several new topical treatments to lower intra-ocular pressure (IOP), considered the major risk factor in glaucoma, have recently been introduced. The agents are more expensive than current drugs, and economic evaluation is therefore required. However, the absence of a final outcome measure makes cost-effectiveness analysis in this disease difficult. There are no epidemiological data that would permit calculation of the annual risk, controlled for age and ocular co-morbidity, of becoming blind, at given levels of intro-ocular pressure (IOP).

This study used an alternative solution by estimating the cost of treatment over one or two years, given the ability of different treatment strategies to control IOP. The consequence of treatment is hence incorporated indirectly, by using clinical data to calculate the proportion of patients who achieve and maintain IOP levels below the desirable clinical target level.

Figure 21 **Structure of the Markov model**

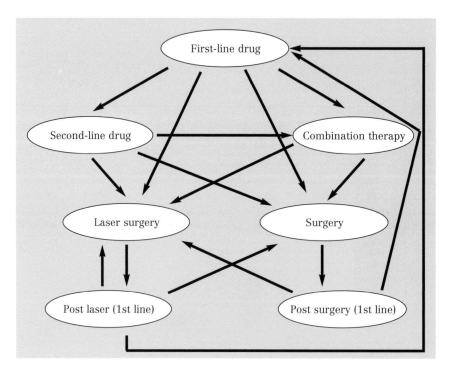

Figure 22 **Distribution of costs by category of resource use (Example: France and UK)**

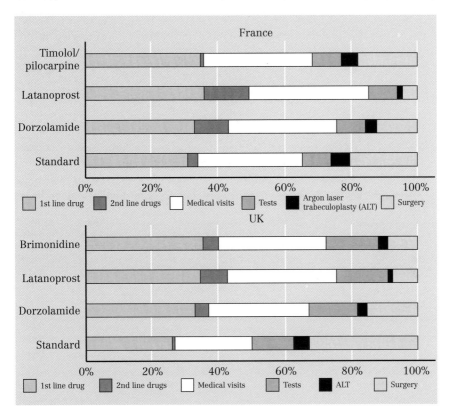

In the Markov model that was used, states are defined by the treatment patients receive rather than by a clinical measure (Figure 21). The cycle length is one month, to account for surgical interventions and follow-up. However, changes to a different treatment can only take place every three months, during a visit, based on the observational study (Study Example 2) where the average time between visits was three months. Changes between treatments in the observational study are directly used to calculate transition probabilities for the base case (current treatment). The effect of the new treatments, approved as second line treatments, was then calculated by replacing the current second-line drugs with the new drugs in the model. The proportions of "controlled patients" at every three-month interval were calculated from clinical trials and used as the new transition probabilities. The cost per cycle was entirely based on resource use in the observational study.

The model found that with the new drugs, the distribution of costs on the different resources changed (Figure 22). With a better control of IOP, the need for surgery decreased and resources were hence shifted from surgery and hospitalization to drug treatment. The net result was that cost did not increase, and, in countries with a high rate of surgery, had the potential to

Table 21 **Average cost per patient during the first year after diagnosis, for intervention with different second-line treatments**

	1st line drug	2nd line drug	Visits	Tests	Argon laser trabeculo-plasty (ALT)	Surgery	Total one year
France (FF)							
Standard							
strategy	739	68	750	211	129	492	2389
2nd line:							
dorzolamide	814	179	751	198	74	289	2305
2nd line:							
latanoprost	753	272	754	186	25	97	2087
2nd line:							
timolol/							
pilocarpine	811	11	751	206	107	419	2305
UK (£)							
Standard							
strategy	69	1	63	33	12	87	265
dorzolamide	70	8	63	31	5	33	210
latanoprost	67	15	63	30	2	15	192
brimonidine	70	9	63	31	5	33	211

decrease for some of the second line treatments, as shown for France and the UK in Table 21.

This study is an example of a model where data from different sources had to be combined, because clinical trials for the new drugs had been against the standard beta-blocker mono-therapy. However, two of the new drugs (latanoprost, dorzolamide) were licensed in second-line use only, and there was hence no clinical trial with a relevant alternative. The calculations are therefore somewhat theoretical and should subsequently be confirmed with actual data.

References

Jönsson B, Krieglstein G (1998) (eds). Primary-open angle glaucoma. Differences in international treatment patterns and cost. Oxford: Isis Medical Media.

Kobelt G, Jönsson L (1999). Modelling cost of patient management with new topical treatments for glaucoma. Results for France and the UK. International Journal of Technology Assessment in Health Care 15(1): 207-219.

Study Example 5 – *Cost-effectiveness of treatment for chronic heart failure*

The prognosis in chronic heart failure (CHF) is poor, with five-year mortality being estimated at 62% and 48% for men and women respectively. Although preventive treatment with ACE-inhibitors has improved survival, one-year mortality in patients with very severe disease (New York Heart Association (NYHA) class IV) remains around 50%. The goal of treatment in CHD is hence to improve survival without, however, increasing morbidity and related hospital inpatient costs (which constitute 60-75% of all costs).

Recently, a new inotropic agent (levosimendan), was shown to significantly improve survival in patients with severe CHD (NYHA III-IV) compared with standard treatment (dobutamine). In a clinical study, 199 patients admitted to cardiac care units in 10 European countries received a 24-hour infusion of either of the two drugs and were followed for one month. Survival was followed-up at six months, but resource utilisation was only available for one month. Hospitalization data were therefore collected retrospectively for the remaining five month period and – probably due to the severity of the disease – it was possible to obtain data for 99% of the patients. Resource utilisation in the economic analysis thus included study drugs and inpatient care. Concomitant medication and outpatient visits were omitted from the analysis, as there was no difference in any of the types of drugs between the two groups and the number of visits was protocol-driven.

In view of there being 10 participating countries, the cost per inpatient day in a cardiology ward, a cardiac care unit and intensive care, and the list price per mg for dobutamine were obtained from each country, transformed into Euro and a mean cost calculated. The price for levosimendan was not yet available and an expected price was assumed for the analysis.

Cost-consequences analysis:
75 of 102 (73.5%) and 61 of 97 (62.9%) patients were alive at six months in the new and standard treatment arms, respectively. Mean survival over six months was 157 days and 139 days. The risk of death was thus reduced by 32% in relative terms and 10.6% in absolute terms with the new treatment. Inpatient costs were similar in the two groups, so the difference between the two groups was entirely due to the study drug (Table 22).

Cost-effectiveness analysis:
In order to capture the full benefit of the improved survival during the one-month trial and six-month follow-up, it is necessary to extrapolate the gain in life expectancy beyond the clinical trial. This requires good epidemiological data for a similar patient group, as survival in CHD depends on age and the severity of the disease. In the CONSENSUS trial (1987), patients with severe CHD were randomised to an ACE-inhibitor or placebo and followed until death (Swedberg et al., 1999). These patients were similar to the patients in the clinical study with levosimendan in terms of age and sex distribution, as well

Table 22 **Resource utilisation and cost over six months**

	Dobutamine	Levosimendan
	Mean (SD)	Mean (SD)
Admissions per patient	2.28 (1.28)	2.33 (1.67)
Inpatient days per patient	29.24 (31.85)	29.46 (30.57)
Hospitalization cost (Euro)	13,933 (12,908)	14,111 (12,712)
Drug cost (Euro)	34 (22)	1,010 (420)
Total costs (Euro)	13,967 (12,902)	15,121 (12,783)
Incremental cost (Euro)		1,154

as one- and six-month mortality (9% versus 11%, 29% versus 31%). As all patients in the levosimendan trial had received ACE-inhibitors, the 10-year follow-up data of the treatment group in CONSENSUS was used for extrapolation of life expectancy.

Blinded follow-up in CONSENSUS was 0.515 years and, at 10 years, five patients were still alive in the ACE-inhibitor group. Conditional mean survival for patients in this group alive at the end of the blinded period was 941 days or 2.6 years (assuming that the five patients still alive after 10 years die immediately). The conditional survival should therefore be interpreted as the lower limit and the actual survival is expected to be higher. Thus, the cost-effectiveness analysis assumed a life-expectancy of three years (discounted at 3% per annum) at the end of the levosimendan trial. Matching survival in the two datasets day per day, the gain in life-expectancy with levosimendan is 0.369 years, as seen in Table 23.

If no patient-level data are available as in this case, the calculation could be done in a simplified way. This is illustrated in Figure 23. Based on the clinical trial, for 100 patients treated in each group, 73.5 would be alive in the levosimendan group and 62.9 in the dobutamine group at six months. The difference in survival is hence 0.0265 [0.5 x (0.5years x 10.6)]. If mean life

Table 23 **Gain in life-expectancy**

	Dobutamine	Levosimendan	Difference
	Mean (SD)	Mean (SD)	
Life years gained (undiscounted)	2.268	2.636	0.369
Life years gained (discounted 3%)	2.133	2.479	0.346

Figure 23 Life-expectancy during and beyond the clinical trial

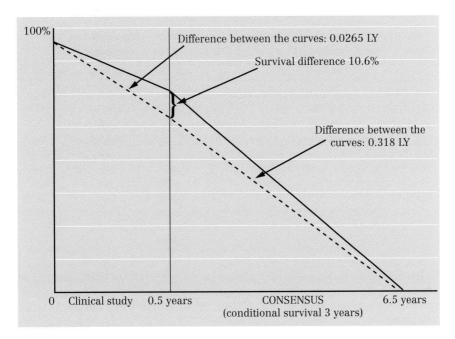

expectancy after the trial is three years, and assuming that survival is linear, the survival gain after the trial is 0.318 [0.5 x (6 years x 10.6)]. The total is then 0.345 years (undiscounted). If the mean life expectancy is only two years, the gain would be 0.239 years on average.

Cost-effectiveness is then calculated as the incremental cost divided by the incremental benefit, as shown in Table 24. CHD is a typical example where costs in added years of life may play a role. Using the data from Johannesson et al. (1997) (Table 25), it was possible in this study to include future costs in the analysis, for the example of Sweden. The cost per life year gained using Swedish costs for hospitalization and drugs is 27,700 SEK (€3,080). When future costs are added, the ratio increases to 190,000 SEK (€21,000).

Table 24 Cost per life year gained

Conditional mean survival	Cost per life year gained (€)
3 years (base case)	3,337
2 years	4,603
4 years	2,639

Table 25 **Annual consumption and production in different age groups in Sweden (SEK 1995)**

Age	Consumption		Production	Consumption minus production
	Private	*Public*		
35-49	98000	32000	214000	– 84000
50-64	113000	32000	182000	– 37000
65 +	77000	82000	0	159000

Source: Johannesson M, Meltzer D, O'Conor R. Incorporating future costs in medical cost-effectiveness analysis: implications for the cost-effectiveness of the treatment of hypertension. Medical Decision Making 1997 17(4):382-389.

References

Cleland J, Takala A, Apajasalo M, Zethraeus N, Kobelt G (2001). Cost-effectiveness of levosimendan in severe low-output heart failure compared to dobutamine based on an international clinical trial (LIDO). Abstract, ISPOR (Cannes, France), November.

Swedberg K, Kjekshus J, Snapinn S, for the consensus investigators (1999). Long term survival in severe heart failure patients treated with enalapril. European Heart Journal 20:136-139.

3.4 Technical issues

The onychomycosis and glaucoma study examples cover a relatively short time frame and both costs and clinical effects were directly available from the clinical trials and other datasets used. The example in heart failure covered a longer time frame involving extrapolation of data beyond the clinical trial, and this study therefore illustrates a number of technical issues in cost-effectiveness analysis.

3.4.1 Time perspective (discounting)

Many economic analyses cover a rather long time frame, and often costs and effects do not occur at the same time. In order to make direct comparisons between treatments, or between expenditures and benefits in different time periods, discounting should be used (Box 6). Discounting can be applied to all forms of economic analyses, and all guidelines request discounting to be done. However, there is some debate about whether both costs and benefits should be discounted or only costs, the argument being that a health benefit does not have a different value, whether it occurs now or at a later time. The general rule is therefore to present results both discounted, using a common rate for costs and effects, and undiscounted. An exception to this is the UK, where

NICE has recommended that submissions by manufacturers and sponsors discount costs and effects at different rates – 6% for costs and 1.5% for health effects.

3.4.2 Future costs (costs in added years of life)

A further technical issue illustrated in the CHD example is the fact that a patient with a life-threatening disease, whose life is saved with a treatment, will continue to use health care resources in the added years of life. In general, only the costs related to the specific disease have been included in cost-effectiveness analyses, and there has been criticism that this over-estimates the cost-effectiveness. Recently, it has been argued that all future related and unrelated costs should be included in the analysis (Meltzer, D. Accounting for future costs in medical cost-effectiveness analysis. Journal of Health Economics 1997,16, 33-64).

Box 6 **Discounting**

Discounting is a technique that allows comparison between costs and benefits that occur at different times. This is particularly important in health care where costs often occur immediately, while benefits may occur at a later stage, for example with preventive programmes such as vaccination, lipid-lowering and anti-hypertensive therapy, or where treatment continues over a long period, for example in the chronic treatment of long-term illness.

Discounting is not a correction for inflation. Rather it reflects time preference, the desire to have benefits earlier rather than later, and the opportunity cost of capital, i.e. the returns that could be gained if the resources were invested elsewhere.

The technique is straightforward. For example, based on a discount rate of 5%, a cost of €1000 occurring in one year's time is considered to be worth only about 95% at present value, i.e. approximately €950. €1000 in two years would be worth €907 today; the same amount in three years would be €864, and so forth. Alternatively, €864 invested at 5% will grow to €1000 in three years' time, and €907 will grow to €1000 in two years' time. The adjustment that has to be made to future flows to express them in present values is:

$$\frac{1}{(1+i)^t}$$

where i is the discount factor and t is the number of years.

Thus, €1000 in 5 years at a discount rate of 6% is worth €747.26 [$1000/(1+0.06)^5$]; €1000 in 10 years has a value of €558.39 today.

Table 26 Lifetime health care costs for people living to 65 or older in the US (Medicare data, US $)

Age at death	Lifetime health care costs	Cost per extra year of life	Cost during the two last years of life
65-70	13000		
71-80	35500	3600	23000
81-90	56000	1200	21000
91-100	63000	400	15000
>100	66000		8000

Source: Lubitz J, Beebe J, Baker C. Longevity and medicare expenditures. N Engl J Med 1995, 332:999-1003

However, to include all health care consumption in the added years of life is not without problems, since it is not entirely obvious that the average consumption can be applied to all age groups, as illustrated in Table 26. While overall expenditures increase as people live longer, expenditure per year as well as expenditures in the last year of life decrease with increasing age.

Also, to make the analysis complete, general consumption and production should also be included as shown in Table 27. In the younger age groups, production is larger than consumption, but the opposite is true after retirement age.

Table 27 illustrates the results of a cost-effectiveness analysis including costs in future years of life. As is illustrated, the effect on the ratios in the younger age groups is minimal, but they change considerably for older people.

3.4.3 Patient groups (stratification of risk)

Another issue in cost-effectiveness analysis is that a treatment may be very cost-effective in one patient group, but not at all in another. When clinical trials are large, patients can be stratified according to their specific risk, as also illustrated in Table 27. The cost per life year saved in younger patients with a low relative risk of a fatal cardiac event (below 45, 90-94 mm Hg diastolic blood pressure) is high, as few events will be avoided in absolute terms, but the ratio will decrease as the risk increases to over 100 mm Hg. The same pattern can be seen in patients aged over 70, but the risk is much higher (at the same blood pressure), and hence the cost per life year saved is substantially lower. As is well known in cardiology, women have a lower risk, which translates directly into higher cost-effectiveness ratios.

3.4.4 Uncertainty (sensitivity analysis and confidence intervals)

Economic evaluations, particularly simulation models, have to rely on different sets of data in order, for instance, to link short or medium term clinical effects (e.g. lowering of hypertension) to the long term outcome (e.g.

Table 27 **Cost per life year gained with and without costs in added years of life through treatment of hypertension in Sweden (1000 SEK 1995, 3% discount rate)**

Diastolic blood pressure	*< 45 years*		*45-69 years*		*> 70 years*	
MmHg	Men	Women	Men	Women	Men	Women
90-94						
– without	818	1825	58	153	29	22
– with	825	1869	161	263	190	182
95-99						
– without	679	1394	29	876	15	7
– with	686	1423	131	204	175	168
100-104						
– without	562	1022	7	36	7	0
– with	569	1051	95	139	168	161

Source: Johannesson, Meltzer, O'Conor 1997

avoidance of stroke), or to incorporate resource utilization. Often, assumptions have to be made to overcome the uncertainty in both the clinical and the resource use data. As the credibility of the results will depend on the quality of the data used, it is important to explore the impact of alternative assumptions and perform extensive sensitivity analysis, particularly for those parameters with the highest degree of uncertainty, as discussed in Box 7.

Box 7 **Sensitivity analysis**

A sensitivity analysis examines the effect on the study results of systematic changes in key assumptions or parameters. For example, what would be the impact on the results if the effectiveness of a treatment is increased or decreased, the cost of any of the resources used is doubled or halved, or the incidence of side effects is lowered or increased? Sensitivity analysis helps to explore some of the uncertainty related to potential variability in the basic data and the sample population, and to extrapolate from one setting to another. It will identify which parameters or assumptions have the most significant effect on the outcome and the stability of the results.

Sensitivity analysis, in its simplest form, involves varying one or more parameters across a possible range. Other variations include finding the threshold value of a variable above or below which the conclusion of the study will change, and analysing the impact of assuming extreme values of a variable.

When data are collected in the context of a trial, the observed variance in the data allows statistical techniques to be applied. Generally, there is a high variability in the data, particularly in costs, and it is becoming standard practice to present confidence intervals for incremental cost-effectiveness ratios. Because the range of estimates for effects can come close to, or sometimes encompass zero, the corresponding range for the cost-effectiveness ratio can approach infinity, and the confidence interval can be extremely wide. One approach which avoids this problem, and which arguably gives a more meaningful indication of the variation in the data, is to calculate cost-effectiveness acceptability curves, as shown in Box 8.

Box 8 **Confidence intervals and cost-effectiveness acceptability curves**

The variability in cost and effect data is often high, leading to incremental cost-effectiveness ratios with a high uncertainty. This variability can be represented statistically in the form of a confidence interval around the incremental cost-effectiveness ratio (ICER). However, because of the properties of the ratio statistic, this is not a straightforward matter.

Different approaches have been developed to estimate confidence intervals for ICERs. Those being used currently include the confidence box-method (e.g. Wakker and Klaassen, 1995), Taylor approximation (delta method, e.g. O'Brien et al., 1994), Fieller's interval method (1954), and bootstrap methods (Briggs et al., 1997). In addition to the possibility that confidence intervals can be extremely wide, their interpretation is complicated by the presence of negative ratios within the interval, since these can have one of two diametrically opposed meanings. Firstly, they can imply that the treatment of interest is more effective and less costly than (dominates) the comparator for some values of costs and effects. Secondly, they can imply that it is more costly and less effective than (is dominated by) the comparator for some values of costs and effects.

A potentially more meaningful way of presenting the same data is the cost-effectiveness acceptability curve, an example of which is given below. This shows, for a range of values of willingness to pay, P, for health benefits, what proportion of estimates of the ICER are acceptable. Using clinical trial data on costs and outcomes, the probability that the ICER falls below the required limit can be derived if an assumption is made about the distributions of mean costs and mean effects. Van Hout et al. (1994) present an illustration assuming normal distributions. Alternatively, the distribution of the ICER may be estimated by bootstrapping from the observed samples. In this approach, bootstrap samples are generated by selecting patients one at a time from the observed data with replacement until a sample the same size as in the original data is obtained. In general, some patients' data will be selected more than once and others' not at all. Taking the mean of costs and effects for this sample gives one bootstrap estimate of mean costs and mean effects. The distributions of mean costs and mean effects, and thus of the ICER, are then estimated by repeating this procedure a large number of times, perhaps several thousands. For a more detailed discussion of the method, the reader is referred to Briggs et al. (1997). Cost-effectiveness acceptability curves can also be estimated

Box 8 **Confidence intervals** *(continued)*

when costs and effects are simulated by a modelling process, for example a Markov model. A distribution for the ICER can be derived using probabilistic sensitivity analysis in which the parameters of the model are assigned distributions and the model is run a large number of times, with resampling from these distributions on each occasion. A detailed illustration of the application of this method is provided by Briggs (2000).

The acceptable range of estimates for the ICER will clearly include all those cases where the treatment of interest dominates the alternative and those cases where the additional cost per unit of health effect is no greater than P. In other words, a new treatment A should replace the old treatment B if the ICER [(costsA-costsB)/(effectsA-effectsB)] is less than or equal to P. The proportion of estimates falling within the threshold P is often interpreted, from a Bayesian perspective, as the probability that the intervention is cost-effective. The figure below illustrates a treatment for which the ICER is below 140,000 US\$ with a 95% probability, and below 60,000 US\$ with an 80% probability.

A statistic which avoids some of the problems of ratios is the net benefit (NB), defined as the monetary value of incremental effects, less incremental costs. The net benefit can therefore be expressed as

$$NB = P \times \Delta \text{ effects} - \Delta \text{ costs}$$

and if it is greater than 0, the new therapy should be adopted.

Plotting the proportion of estimates for which the NB is positive against different values of P gives an equivalent presentation to the cost-effectiveness acceptability curve.

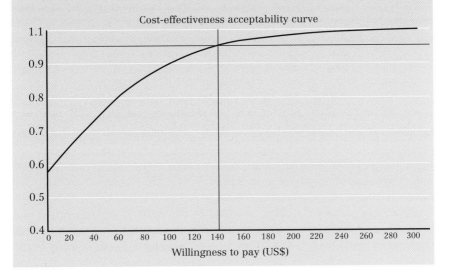

Cost-effectiveness acceptability curve

Summary of cost-effectiveness analysis:

- **A cost-effectiveness analysis considers both cost and effects of treatments and compares them.**

- **Treatment effects, i.e. outcomes, are measured in natural units (life years saved, patients cured, etc.).**

- **The results are expressed as ratios of additional costs over additional health effects – i.e. incremental cost-effectiveness ratios or ICERs.**

- **The uncertainty in the data used for the analysis is evaluated with extensive sensitivity or statistical analysis.**

3.5 Cost-minimization analysis

Cost-minimization analysis is a special type of cost-effectiveness analysis used when two or more health care interventions have the same outcomes. In such a case, and provided that there is conclusive evidence that the treatments being evaluated have indeed the same effectiveness and there is no, or no consequential, difference in health outcome, the analysis can be limited to the costs only. A decision-maker who is responsible for all relevant costs will choose the treatment with the lowest total cost. By doing so, resources will be used efficiently.

Cost-minimization analyses are rather infrequent, as it is rare that two treatments have identical outcomes. This is particularly the case for new treatments, as the very reason for developing these is to improve outcomes. However, often new formulations of existing drugs, new methods of administering treatments or technical improvements in procedures may fundamentally change the cost structure of health care interventions, without affecting the outcomes.

For instance, a large number of surgical interventions which have traditionally been performed as inpatient procedures are now undertaken on an outpatient basis, due to improvements in anaesthetic and surgical techniques. Frequently, the outcome of surgery is identical whether performed on an inpatient or an outpatient basis. However, hospitalization costs will differ significantly for the two alternatives, and hence the two types of surgery can be compared on a cost-minimization basis. The technique of cost-minimization analysis is shown in Box 9.

Another example one can think of would be the route of administration of a drug. Giving a drug via intravenous infusion, intramuscular or subcutaneous injection or orally will carry different costs. Within these, differences in the duration of an infusion, in the number of injections needed during a day, the

Box 9 **Theoretical example of cost-minimization analysis for illustrative purposes**

Medicine A and medicine B both reduce one-year mortality from 25% to 15%, at a price of €10,000 and €20,000, respectively.

Medicine A requires careful dose-titration in an inpatient setting and monthly laboratory tests, whereas medicine B is taken orally and requires yearly laboratory testing.

Additional hospitalization and laboratory costs for A are estimated at €12,000, those for B at €500.

Total costs for medicine A are €10,000 + €12,000 = €22,000

Total costs for medicine B are €20,000 + €500 = €20,500

Alternative B, despite its acquisition cost being double that of alternative A, reduces total costs by €1,500.

need for injections by a health care professional compared to self-injection, etc., will influence costs.

Study Example 6 – *Kidney transplantation*

Transplantation in the treatment of chronic renal failure has been shown to be less costly and more effective than dialysis. Addition of cyclosporin A to the immuno-suppressive regimen was subsequently shown in several analyses to improve short and long term graft survival and to reduce total costs of transplantation by reducing hospitalization costs. The pharmacokinetic profile of cyclosporin A, however, required close monitoring of plasma levels, in order to maintain immunosuppression at an optimal level and avoid costly episodes of graft rejection at low plasma levels, or adverse effects of the medicine at high plasma levels. A new galenical form of cyclosporin A was shown to have a linear and predictable pharmacokinetic profile, and plasma levels within the optimal therapeutic window were found to be easier to achieve. This should lead to a further improvement in the efficiency of performing transplantations, particularly during the early months after transplantation.

Resource use in a three month double-blind clinical trial in de novo transplant patients, comparing the two galenical forms of cyclosporin A, was analysed retrospectively in four countries. The clinical outcome in this trial – graft survival – was expected to be identical for both groups and a cost-minimization analysis was therefore undertaken. The perspective of the analysis was that of a hospital, and only direct hospital costs were included. A cost advantage was shown for the new galenical form, with the savings mainly due to a reduced need to monitor

Figure 24 **Retrospective cost analysis of managing de novo transplant patients (Figures in Swiss Francs)**

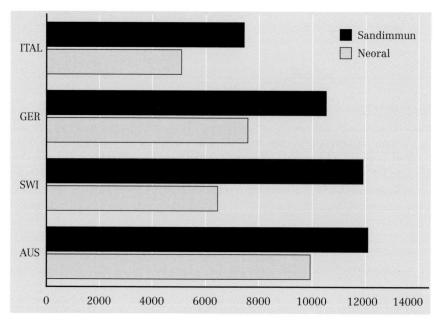

Source: Hardens et al., Poster, Pharmacoeconomic Conference, May 1994, Ghent, Belgium

rejection episodes, i.e. fewer concomitant immunosuppressive medicines and shorter hospitalizations (Hardens et al., 1994), as illustrated in Figure 24.

From a strictly methodological point of view, the results of this analysis should be considered as indicative only, as the number of patients in the trial was small and the follow-up short. Observational studies to assess the cost-savings in a normal practice setting (although treatment protocols in transplantation are generally not different between clinical trials and normal practice) and over a longer period of time would be required to confirm these data.

Reference

Hardens et al. (1994), Poster, Pharmacoeconomic Conference, Ghent, Belgium, May 1994.

Summary of cost-minimization analysis:

- **Cost-minimization analysis is the term applied to an economic evaluation when two or more treatment alternatives produce identical health outcomes.**

- **Only the costs borne reaching the outcome are analysed, and often only direct medical costs are considered.**

- **The treatment with the lowest cost is preferred.**

3.6 Cost-utility analysis

3.6.1 Introduction

Much of modern medicine is concerned with improving the quality, not the duration, of life. Therefore, the effects on patients' quality of life of different healthcare interventions need to be considered together with survival or other clinical measures if the total impact of treatment on a patient is to be gauged. A number of outcome measures have been designed to include both these concepts, such as the healthy year equivalent (HYE), the disability-adjusted life year (DALY) and the quality-adjusted life year (QALY). The QALY is by far the most frequently used measure today. DALYs have essentially only been used in international comparative studies by the World Bank and the World Health Organisation and have been advanced principally as a means of estimating the overall burden of disease in terms of DALYs lost. The relatively onerous demands placed on respondents by the HYE method help to explain why it has been infrequently adopted in economic evaluations.

Cost-utility analysis is a type of cost-effectiveness analysis that incorporates both quantity and quality of life, by estimating the cost per QALY gained. QALYs are calculated by weighting time (years of life) with a quality-adjustment, called utility (see below), which represents the relative preference values that individuals or society place on different states of health.

Cost-utility analysis has two major advantages compared to other economic evaluation techniques. In addition to combining life expectancy and overall quality of life aspects, the use of a standard outcome measure allows for comparison between the cost-effectiveness of treatments in different disease areas with very different clinical outcome measures. A payer for health care, for instance a national health service, will need to compare different interventions in order to decide on expenditures and prioritize within the budget. It is therefore not surprising that organizations such as NICE prefer cost-utility analysis to other types of analyses. As economic evaluation per se does not give a value to the benefit itself, but only estimates the inputs required to reach a given outcome, comparison is an essential feature of resource allocation. Therefore, a number of "league tables" of different health care interventions have been created, as illustrated in Table 28. In practice, however, such league tables have to be considered with caution, as often the methodology used in cost-utility evaluations is not consistent between studies (Mason et al., 1993), making comparisons questionable. For instance, studies may use different concepts of costs, or be performed from different perspectives and thus include or exclude different types of resources. They may also estimate utilities using different methods, and it has been shown that there can be differences between the values generated by the various methods. For example, the standard gamble tends to give slightly higher values than the time trade-off, and both of these will

Table 28 'League Table' – Cost per quality-adjusted life year for selected interventions in the UK

Treatment	Cost per QALY (Aug 1990 £s)
Cholesterol testing and diet therapy (40-69 years)	220
Advice to stop smoking from GP	270
Antihypertensive treatment to prevent stroke (45-64 years)	490
Pacemaker implantation	1100
Hip replacement	1180
Cholesterol testing and treatment	1480
Coronary Artery Bypass Graft (CABG) (left main vessel disease, severe angina)	2090
Kidney transplant	4710
Breast cancer screening	5780
Heart transplantation	7840
Cholesterol testing and treatment (incrementally), all adults 25-39	14150
Home haemodialysis	17260
CABG (one vessel disease, moderate angina)	18830
Hospital haemodialysis	21970
Erythropoietin treatment for anaemia in dialysis patients (mortality –10%)	54380
Erythropoietin treatment for anaemia in dialysis patients (no incremental survival)	126290

Source: Modified from Maynard (1991)

generally give lower values than a visual analogue scale. These methods, as well as preference instruments, are explained below.

3.6.2 Utilities

In economic evaluation, utilities are preference weights for given health states, where one generally represents full health and zero represents death. There are basically two types of methods to calculate utilities. Either preference values for health states are directly elicited from patients in an interview, or preference-based generic quality of life questionnaires such as the EQ-5D (EuroQol) or the HUI (Health Utility Index) are used. In the first case, when an empirical investigation is being undertaken, patients enrolled in the study are asked to rate scenarios relating to their health and the treatment they receive, using one of the valuation methods described below (e.g. standard gamble). These values are then used to rate the quality of life benefits of treatment. A variation on this approach would be to ask health care professionals or other relevant respondents to undertake the valuation exercise. When an evaluation involves a simulated group of patients (a decision analysis model, for example), the analyst may select a group of patients representative of those to which the analysis is intended to apply. In contrast, the quality of life

Table 29 **The five dimensions of the EQ-5D**

Dimension	Levels
Mobility	No problems walking about
	Some problems walking about
	Confined to bed
Self-care	No problems with self-care
	Some problems washing or dressing self
	Unable to wash or dress self
Usual activities	No problems with performing usual activities (e.g. work, study, housework, family or leisure activities)
	Some problems with performing usual activities
	Unable to perform usual activities
Pain/discomfort	No pain or discomfort
	Moderate pain or discomfort
	Extreme pain or discomfort
Anxiety/depression	Not anxious or depressed
	Moderately anxious or depressed
	Extremely anxious or depressed

instruments mentioned as candidates in the second approach have a pre-defined set of scores associated with them. These instruments provide a utility rating that can be used directly to calculate QALYs. For example, a 'tariff' has been generated for the EQ-5D in the UK using a time trade-off exercise among a random sample of the general public (Dolan et al, 1995). Analysts may therefore assign a value to the health status associated with any set of responses to the EQ-5D questionnaire by reference to the tariff. In collectively financed health care systems, it is argued that the general population is the most appropriate group to provide valuations which could influence the allocation of resources between different programmes across the health service.

The HUI (Torrance et al., 1996) originates in Canada and is frequently used in North America. The EQ-5D (Dolan et al., 1995) was developed in Europe and appears currently to be the most frequently used instrument, because as a simple generic questionnaire measure it can be used in virtually any study, be it cross-sectional surveys or clinical trials. In addition, it has been translated into a large number of languages. It is a two-part measure that provides both a compact descriptive profile and a single index value. The descriptive part addresses five dimensions of health (see Table 29) at three degrees of perceived problems coded as 1 (no problem), 2 (some problem), and 3 (severe

Figure 25 **The visual analogue scale in the EQ-5D**

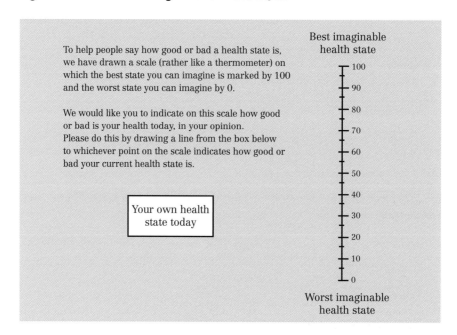

problems). Individual responses from each of the five dimensions define one of 243 theoretically possible health states. For example, state 11111 indicates no problem in any of the domains and is equivalent to full health. Utility values for a representative sample of the 243 health states were assessed with the time trade-off method in the general population in the UK, and a full health state classification system was developed. In addition, the EQ-5D contains a visual analogue scale in the form of a thermometer (see Figure 25).

When it is possible to elicit preference weights directly from patient groups in an interview, several techniques can be used, such as:

- the **Standard Gamble (SG)** (Figure 26), a classical technique that is implied by the axioms of expected utility theory and used to measure the utility that an individual attaches to any given health state; the technique has also been extensively used in decision analysis to assess the closely related issue of risk aversion.

- the **Time Trade-off (TTO)** (Figure 27), developed in the early 1970s specifically for use in health care.

- **Visual Analogue Scales (VAS)** (Figure 28), the simplest method for eliciting health state 'utilities', where individuals are asked to indicate where on a line between the best and worst imaginable health states they would rate a pre-defined intermediate health state. The EQ-5D thermometer (Figure 25) is an example of a VAS.

Figure 26 **Standard gamble**

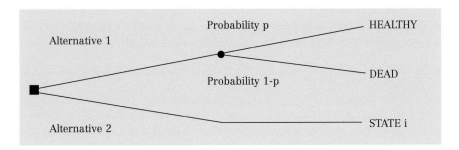

In a typical standard gamble scenario, an individual is offered two alternatives:

- *Alternative 1* has two possible outcomes: either return to full health for the remaining years of life expectancy with a probability of *p*, or experience immediate death with a probability of *(1-p)*.

- *Alternative 2* has one certain outcome of a chronic health state *i* for the remaining years of life expectancy.

The individual is then allowed to vary the probability, *p*, until she/he is indifferent between the two alternatives. If full health and death are automatically assigned utilities of one and zero respectively, then the utility for state *i* is given by *p*. (At the point of indifference between the two alternatives, p(1) + (1-p)(0) = utility of health state i. Therefore, the utility of health state i = p.)

As in the standard gamble, in the time trade-off method an individual is offered two alternatives: Alternative 1 is full health for time *x (x < t)* followed by death. Alternative 2 is to remain in health state i for time *t* (life expectancy

Figure 27 **Time trade-off**

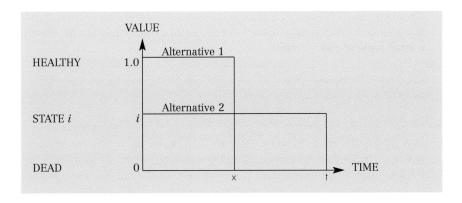

for that condition) followed by death. Time x is then varied until the individual is indifferent between the two alternatives, at which point the utility for state i is given by x/t.

- *Alternative 1* is full health for time *x* followed by death.

- *Alternative 2* is to remain in intermediate health state *i* for time *t (t > x)* followed by death.

The individual is then allowed to vary time *x* until she/he is indifferent between the two alternatives. If full health and death are assigned utilities of one and zero respectively, then the utility for health state *i* is given by *x/t*. (At the point of indifference between the two alternatives, x(1) = t * utility of health state i. Therefore, the utility of health state i = x/t.)

Figure 28 **Visual analogue scale (VAS)**

With Visual Analogue Scales (VAS), individuals are asked to indicate where on the line between the best and worst imaginable state they would rate a certain health state (their own or a described state). The health state valuation is then derived by measuring the distances between healthy (generally assigned 1) or dead (generally assigned 0 if it is regarded as the worst imaginable state) and the indicated health state on the line. On, for example, a 10 cm line with death at 0 and full health at 10 cm, a health state indicated as being located 8 cm along the line would receive a score of 0.8 (8/10).

The basic techniques of a cost-utility analysis are shown with a hypothetical example in Box 10.

Box 10 **Theoretical example of cost utility analysis for illustrative purposes**

Treatment A gives a survival of 1 year at a quality of life (utility) of 0.7, at a cost of €1,400.

Treatment B improves survival to 1.2 years, but reduces quality of life (utility) to 0.6, at a cost of €2,160.

The average cost-utility of A is €2,000 per QALY (€1,400 / {0.7 x 1})
The average cost-utility of B is €3,000 per QALY (€2,160 / {0.6 x 1.2})

The incremental cost-utility of B over A is €38,000 per QALY ({2,160-1,400} / {0.72-0.7})

Summary of cost-utility analysis:

- **A cost-utility analysis considers both costs and effects of treatment**

- **It integrates both patients' life-expectancy and health related quality of life in the outcome measure**

- **Effects (outcomes) are expressed as quality-adjusted life years (QALYs)**

- **QALYs are calculated by adjusting life-expectancy by its quality (utility)**

- **Utilities express a preference for a given health state, generally between zero (dead) and one (full health)**

- **The results of cost-utility analyses in difference disease areas with different clinical outcomes can be compared**

- **Published league tables of various cost-utility studies have to be interpreted and used with the greatest caution**

Study Example 7 – *Osteoporosis*

Osteoporosis is characterized by low bone mass, which implies that the risk of fractures increases. The increased fracture risk leads to consequences for both the individual and for society as a whole. Common osteoporosis related fractures are fractures of the hip, wrist and spine that can lead to reductions in the individual's quality of life and in some cases also an increased mortality risk. Societal costs that can be attributed to osteoporosis are costs for prevention and treatment and costs associated with fractures.

Early economic evaluations of preventive treatments were based on changes in bone mineral density (BMD), which was then linked with an epidemiological risk function for fractures at a given age and level of BMD. Since the early nineties, fracture studies are required to license a treatment, and the cost of events (fractures) avoided could be calculated directly. However, the reason to avoid fractures is to avoid the morbidity and mortality associated with fractures, and cost per event avoided does therefore not reflect the true outcome. In addition, current treatments in osteoporosis can affect multiple endpoints, for example several different types of fractures, or extra-skeletal consequences. An example of this is hormone replacement therapy (HRT). HRT treatment is thought not only to reduce the risk of fractures, but also to decrease the risk of heart disease (CHD) and conversely to increase the risk of breast cancer.

To estimate the cost-effectiveness of such an intervention that affects several types of events requires a model where the risks of all relevant events are included. Also, the outcome measure must capture all the different consequences for morbidity and mortality for these events.

Figure 29 **Model structure**

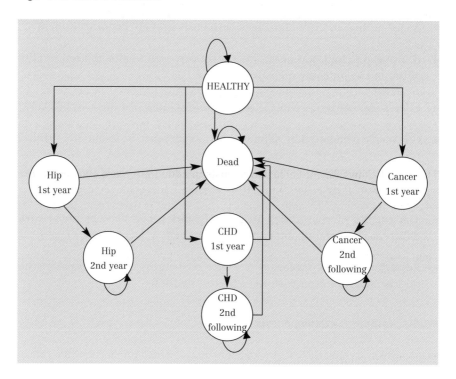

Such a model is presented in this example (Zethraeus et al., 1999). The Markov model allows the cost per QALY of HRT in the prevention/treatment of postmenopausal women's health problems to be estimated. The model's overall structure and the Markov states are shown in Figure 29.

Each state is associated with age-dependent mortality rates, costs and quality of life (utility) weights, and the model runs in annual cycles. The disease states are divided into "first year" and "second and following years" after a disease event since mortality rates, costs, and quality of life differ between these time periods. Costs and utilities for the different states are shown in Tables 30 and 31 respectively.

The basic model structure assumes a cohort of healthy individuals, i.e. free of CHD and breast cancer and with no previous fracture. After each cycle, the cohort is reallocated to the different health states according to the transition probabilities. In the first cycle the cohort is exposed to the risks of CHD, breast cancer, hip fractures and death from other causes. When a patient experiences an event, only transitions to "second and following years" (post-event state) or "death" are relevant. Patients in the states "second and following years" remain in these states until they die. The cohort is followed until age 110. The cost-effectiveness formula used in the computer model can be expressed as:

$$\frac{\Delta C}{\Delta E} = \frac{C_1 - C_0}{E_1 - E_0} = \frac{\Delta INT + \Delta MORB + \Delta MORT}{\Delta QLE} = \frac{\Delta INT + \Delta MORB + \Delta MORT}{\Delta LE + \Delta LEQ}$$

where

ΔINT = intervention costs, direct and indirect

$\Delta MORB$ = changes in morbidity costs (direct, indirect) due to the intervention

$\Delta MORT$ = changes in mortality costs (direct, indirect) due to the intervention

ΔLE = changes in life expectancy due to the intervention

ΔLEQ = changes in quality of life measured in years due to the intervention

$\Delta QLE = \Delta LE + \Delta LEQ$.

The model allows for the inclusion of costs in added life years and results are expressed either as costs per life year gained (LYG) or costs per quality-adjusted life year (QALY) gained. As the model incorporates consequences for different diseases, effectiveness measures, such as number of events avoided from an intervention, do not provide meaningful information. Instead a composite outcome measure is needed, which incorporates the intervention's effectiveness for different risks.

Costs in all states include direct and indirect costs. Annual intervention costs (ΔINT) include the cost of drugs, costs for services in hospitals and primary

Table 30 **Costs ($) used in the model**

Age	Type of cost	Acute myocardial infarction (AMI) (recog-nised)	AMI (un-recog-nised)	Angina pectoris	Coronary in-suffic-iency	Hip fracture	Breast cancer	Cost/ LYG
		First year						
50-64	Direct	6,250	437	6,250	10,625	9,875	8,375	–4,625
	Indirect	11,250	3,437	11,250	11,250	10,000	10,375	–
65-74	Direct	6,250	437	6,250	10,625	10,750	8,375	19,875
	Indirect	0	0	0	0	0	0	–
75-84	Direct	6,250	437	6,250	10,625	18,875	8,375	19,875
	Indirect	0	0	0	0	0	0	–
85-	Direct	6,250	437	6,250	10,625	26,375	8,375	19,875
	Indirect	0	0	0	0	0	0	–
		Second year and following						
50-85-	Direct	875	437	875	875	5,125	150	–
50-64	Indirect	6,875	3,437	6,875	6,875	7,000	175	–
65+	Indirect	0	0	0	0	0	0	–

Table 31 **Utility weights used in the model**

Age	Cardiovascular disease*	Hip fracture	Breast cancer	Population
	First year			
50-64	0.8	0.7	0.8	0.9
65-74	0.69	0.59	0.69	0.79
75-	0.53	0.43	0.53	0.63
	Second year and following			
50-64	0.8	0.8	0.8	0.9
65-74	0.69	0.69	0.69	0.79
75-	0.53	0.53	0.53	0.63

*Includes AMI (recognised and unrecognised), angina and coronary insufficiency

health care, travelling costs and production forgone due to the treatment (indirect costs). These latter costs are particularly relevant for primary prevention where "healthy time" is used for the intervention (e.g. physician visits). In addition, there is an "initial cost" for the intervention, e.g. costs for screening or diagnosis. Changes in morbidity costs ($\Delta MORB$) are costs saved

Table 32 **Cost-utility of 10-year intervention with HRT in asymptomatic women. Costs per life year and quality-adjusted life year (QALY) gained (QALYin parentheses) (1000 SEK)**

	Oestrogen (Hysterectomised women)			Oestrogen+Progestogen (Intact uterus)		
	Age			Age		
Risk change	50	60	70	50	60	70
Hip –40%, CHD –20%	400 (310)	240 (230)	170 (190)	580 (450)	300 (300)	200 (230)
Hip –40%, CHD –50%	160 (140)	170 (190)	160 (200)	230 (200)	200 (220)	180 (220)
Hip –50%, CHD –20%	360 (280)	210 (200)	150 (170)	540 (410)	280 (260)	180 (200)
Hip –50%, CHD –50%	150 (120)	160 (170)	150 (180)	220 (190)	190 (200)	170 (200)
Hip–40%, CHD–20%, Cancer+35%	D (640)	270 (240)	170 (190)	D (1060)	370 (320)	210 (230)
Hip–40%, CHD–50%, Cancer+35%	190 (130)	180 (180)	160 (200)	320 (230)	210 (220)	180 (220)
Hip–50%, CHD–20%, Cancer+35%	D (500)	240 (200)	150 (160)	D (860)	330 (280)	180 (200)
Hip–50%, CHD–50%, Cancer+35%	170 (120)	170 (170)	150 (180)	300 (210)	200 (200)	170 (200)

D = HRT is dominated by the no intervention alternative

because of reduced morbidity from CHD and hip fractures and costs added because of increased morbidity from breast cancer. Changes in mortality costs (Δ*MORT*) are equal to changes in total consumption minus production, due to a change in mortality from the intervention.

An example of using this model to investigate the cost-effectiveness of HRT given to asymptomatic women for 10 years is shown in Table 32 (Zethraeus et al., 1999). Depending on uterus status and age (50,60,70), six independent treatment groups were identified. The annual average intervention cost was estimated at SEK 2000.

Reference

Zethraeus N, Johannesson M, Jönsson B (1999). A computer model to analyse the cost-effectiveness of hormone replacement therapy. International Journal of Technology Assessment in Health Care 15(2): 352-365.

Study Example 8 – *Cost-utility in rheumatoid arthritis*

In fields such as osteoporosis or cardiovascular disease, the goal of treatment is to control a risk in order to avoid an event sometime in the future (e.g. control of bone mineral density to avoid osteoporotic fractures, or of blood pressure and cholesterol levels to avoid cardiac events). Economic evaluation can therefore be based on clear endpoints. In chronic progressive diseases, such as rheumatoid arthritis (RA) or multiple sclerosis (MS), the goal of treatment is to alleviate symptoms and slow progression of the disease, hence there is no obvious clinical measure that could be used as an outcome in economic evaluation. However, such diseases carry a considerable economic burden, as onset is relatively early, the effect on quality of life is substantial and patients live with the disease for a long time. Economic evaluation to evaluate the effect of slowing progression is thus important, and the QALY appears the most appropriate and comprehensive effectiveness measure.

Typically, clinical trials will be too short to estimate the benefit of slowing progression, and the effects from the trial must again be extrapolated to the future. This requires a description of the disease progress in terms that are relevant for economic evaluation and an outcome measure that encompasses all different symptoms of the disease. One way to describe disease processes is to use Markov models, provided good epidemiological data are available, and the QALY appears to be the best way to describe the outcome, as it captures overall quality of life over a given time frame.

A recent study has demonstrated how such a disease model can be developed for RA and used to calculate the cost-effectiveness of treatments that affect disease progression (Kobelt et al., 1999). The initial five-year model has been updated with 15-year data and the new model is used to estimate the cost-effectiveness of new treatments in RA, using the example of infliximab (Kobelt et al., forthcoming).

Table 33 **Cohort distribution in the disease states (percent of patients)**

Disease state	Percent of patients									
	Year 1	Year 2	Year 3	Year 4	Year 5	Year 6	Year 7	Year 8	Year 9	Year 10
1	34	36	36	35	26	29	34	32	30	28
2	38	31	31	28	40	33	24	25	25	28
3	14	25	25	23	26	27	24	27	23	23
4	9	4	5	10	5	8	16	12	17	13
5	4	3	3	3	2	2	2	4	4	4
6	1	0	1	1	0	0	0	1	0	3

The model:
The model is based on a Swedish cohort study where 183 patients with early RA were followed for up to 15 years. Both functional and radiological measures were available to define Markov states, but the model was only based on the functional scores measured with the Health Assessment Questionnaire (HAQ), as:

a) the HAQ is used in all clinical trials and the model can thus be used with new clinical data, while radiological scores of the major joints are not always measured in short-term clinical trials;

b) the HAQ correlated well with patients' quality of life assessed with a simple visual analogue scale, as well as with resource utilization, while radiological scores did not.

In this model, contrary to models in osteoporosis, cardiology, or MS (see next study example), disease states are based on a subjective measure rather than on the objective clinical endpoint of joint destruction. Table 33 illustrates the progression of the disease over 10 years, as more patients are in the more severe states 3 to 6, and fewer in the milder states 1-2 (excluding those patients who died). The model included normal mortality.

Cycles in the model are one year, and disease progression is modelled as annual transitions between the states, conditional upon time (i.e. annual cycles elapsed) and patient characteristics such as age, sex, and time since disease onset, using a probit model.

Costs and utilities:
Costs and utilities differ between states, but are constant for all patients within the same state, irrespective of age, gender or other factors. Costs for inpatient care, surgical interventions, outpatient visits, medication and drug monitoring were taken directly from the cohort study, as was sick leave and early retirement, but expenses borne by patients themselves were not available.

Table 34 **Costs (per one-year cycle) and utilities for the different states (SEK)**

State	Utilities	Direct costs					Indirect costs	Total costs
		Inpatient	Surgery	Outpatient	Medication	Total direct		
1	0.73	4864	498	1803	425	7590	0	7590
2	0.64	10012	812	2155	597	13577	62967	76544
3	0.61	16304	1054	2289	556	20203	89498	109701
4	0.42	33148	2073	2469	861	38551	163672	202223
5	0.24	29935	1973	2355	1053	35316	260804	296120
6	0.22	17029	0	1602	77	18707	284204	302911

Work capacity in state 1, where there is basically no disability, was used as the reference, and indirect costs for the other states calculated as the difference from state 1. Utilities for different levels of HAQ were assessed in a special cross-sectional survey with the EQ-5D. Table 34 shows costs and utilities by Markov state.

Table 35 **Cost per QALY gained of infliximab (SEK, discounted 3%)**

Scenario	Infliximab	Placebo	Difference
Model A (one year treatment)			
Direct cost	257 826	191 857	65 969
Total cost	1 129 507	1 121 476	8 031
Utility	4.632	4.384	0.248
Cost/QALY, direct costs			266 000
Cost/QALY, all costs			32 000
Model B (one year treatment)			
Direct cost	266 757	212 391	54 366
Total cost	1 187 780	1 250 406	–62626
Utility	4.648	4.417	0.231
Cost/QALY, direct costs			235 000
Cost/QALY, all costs			(cost-saving)
Model B (one year including loss of effect at treatment discontinuation)			
Direct cost	270 774	212 391	58 383
Total cost	1 219 365	1 250 406	–31 041
Utility	4.596	4.417	0.179
Cost/QALY, direct costs			325 000
Cost/QALY, all costs			(cost-saving)

Figure 30 **Average development of HAQ scores in the model, adjusted for different effectiveness after a one-year trial (lower HAQ values indicate less disability)**

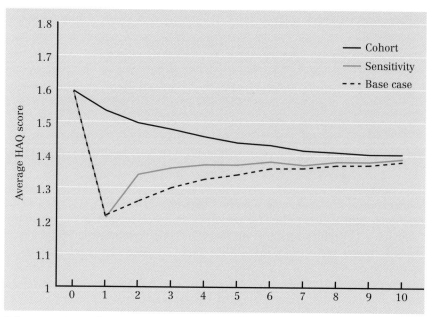

Cohort: transitions from the epidemiological study.

Base case: the treatment effect of infliximab (Remicade) is maintained when treatment is stopped and patients follow the transitions of the epidemiological cohort.

Sensitivity analysis: some of the treatment effect is lost within the year following treatment cessation, after which patients follow the transitions of the epidemiological cohort.

Simulations:

The model allows costs and QALYs to be estimated for a defined number of years for patients with different levels of disability at onset. For instance, patients starting in state 1 will have cumulative costs over 10 years of 573,500 SEK (SD 621,500; €60,500) and 5.479 QALYs (SD 0.666; both discounted at 3%), illustrating the large reduction in quality of life and substantial costs of the disease.

The model was used to estimate the cost-effectiveness of infliximab, a new treatment for RA, based on an international clinical trial. The study included 428 patients, and HAQ scores from the blinded part of the trial were available for 1 year. There are two possible ways to use such data in a Markov model:

1) Treatment and placebo groups from the trial are modelled first, using the same methodology as the model, and then extrapolated to 10 years using data from the Swedish cohort (Model A).

2) The difference between the treatment and placebo groups is used to calculate odds-ratios of worsening or improvement and these are then applied to the cohort study (Model B).

The choice between the two will mostly depend on the number of patients in the clinical trial and the quality of the data. In this case, both methods were used and gave very similar results. Table 35 shows the cost-effectiveness over 10 years of one-year treatment with infliximab from a societal perspective (both models), as well as a sensitivity analysis for a potential partial loss of effect when treatment is stopped (model B), as illustrated hypothetically in Figure 30.

References

Kobelt, G, Jönsson L, Eberhardt K, Jönsson B (1999). Economic consequences of the progression of rheumatoid arthritis in Sweden. Arthritis And Rheumatism 42(2): 347-56.

Kobelt G, Jönsson L, Lindgren P, Eberhardt K, Young A. The cost-effectiveness of infliximab in the treatment of rheumatoid arthritis in Sweden and the United Kingdom, based on the ATTRACT trial. (forthcoming, British Journal of Rheumatology).

Kobelt G, Jönsson L, Lindgren P, Eberhardt K, Young A. Economic progression of rheumatoid arthritis in Sweden and in the United Kingdom. (forthcoming, Arthritis and Rheumatism).

Study Example 9 – *Cost-utility in multiple sclerosis*

Compared to RA, multiple sclerosis is a more difficult disease to model. It shares all the issues of RA, but symptoms are much more diverse and, in addition to progression of disability, there are distinct events (exacerbations) where functional disability becomes extreme during a more or less limited amount of time. This has led to two main definitions of the disease, relapsing-remitting MS (RRMS) and secondary progressive (SPMS), but the transition from the first to the second is not well defined. Most of the new agents to treat MS are licensed for RRMS, as they have been shown to reduce the number and severity of relapses, but only one drug is approved for use in SPMS. This poses the problem of modelling two distinct phases of a disease, as well as the link between the two, as the goal of treatment is to avoid progression to severe disability where costs are high and quality of life is low.

Several different models have been developed by different authors. The example presented here was initially developed for SPMS and uses the extensive resource utilisation and utility data presented in Study Example 1 in this book. The first version (Kobelt et al., 2000) was entirely based on clinical data, the second version (Kobelt et al., 2002) incorporated natural history data, and the latest version combines RRMS and SPMS (Kobelt et al., 2001). This illustrates how such models can continue to be adapted and improved, as new knowledge develops and more data become available. The modelling approach is similar to the RA model in Study Example 8. The model has six

Table 36 Cost and utilities for three months by levels of disability in Sweden

| State | Mean 3-month costs (SEK, 1999) | | | | Utility |
	Direct	Indirect	Informal	Total	EQ-5D
1	8957	126	20109	29192	0.677
2	19566	3611	30312	53489	0.534
3	27991	2675	28508	59174	0.544
4	50098	4756	40480	95334	0.418
5	97697	5417	39746	142860	0.210
6	149942	14352	56696	220990	–0.027*

*Set to 0 in the model

Markov states based on a measure of functional disability (Extended Disability Status Scale (EDSS), assessed by physicians) and one state for dead. EDSS scores correlate well with resource utilisation and quality of life, regardless of the type of MS and the country (see Study Example 1). Swedish values for the Markov states are shown in Table 36.

The first three years in the SPMS model are directly based on a large clinical trial with Betaferon, where 718 patients were followed for three years, regardless of whether they withdrew from treatment or not, and quarterly EDSS scores assessed. Such a trial is powerful enough to estimate transition probabilities between the states, at each three-month interval, separately for patients with or without a relapse during the quarter, as well as to assess compliance with treatment. The structure of the model is shown in Figure 31.

Figure 31 **The structure of the Markov model**

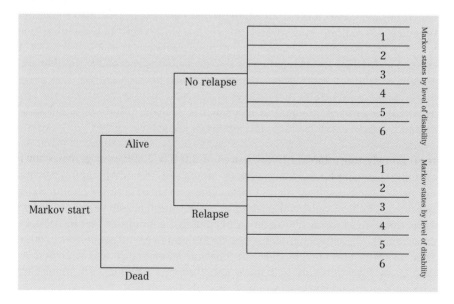

Table 37 Cost per QALY with three-year treatment (direct, indirect and informal care costs included)

	10-year model (costs and QALYs discounted 3%)		
	Incremental cost	QALY gain	Cost per QALY gained (SEK/QALY)
3 year treatment, all costs included			
SPMS, extrapolation based on clinical trial	55 500	0.162	342 600
SPMS, extrapolation based on natural history cohort	55 770	0.217	257 000
RRMS and SPMS, active patients extrapolation based on natural history cohort	13 700	0.207	66 200

Initially, extrapolation beyond the trial was based on mean progression and relapse rates in the placebo group during the clinical trial. This is frequently done when no epidemiological data are available, and the rates are then modified in a sensitivity analysis. Over a 10-year period, the cost per QALY gained with a three-year intervention was estimated at 342,600 SEK (Table 37).

Subsequently, data for 824 patients in a 30-year natural history database was incorporated into the model. When combining such datasets, it is important to assess the similarity of the patient population. In this analysis, patients were similar in terms of age at diagnosis, disease duration, time to conversion from RRMS to SPMS and EDSS score at conversion. Combining the two databases was hence not problematic, the less so as transition probabilities between states were calculated conditional upon these characteristics. When the natural history data are used to extrapolate beyond the clinical trial, the cost per QALY gained decreases to 257,000 SEK (Table 37).

The reason for this is that the clinical trial extrapolation underestimated disease progression, as can be seen in Figure 32. There are several explanations for this, the major one being the type of patients enrolled in the trial, namely those having EDSS scores of 3.0-5.5. Epidemiology has shown that patients will plateau for quite some time at EDSS 6.0, before progression to 7.0 (wheelchair). As a consequence, there will be a limited number of patients in a three-year trial who progress beyond 6.0, and using these data for extrapolation will project this "plateau-effect" forward and underestimate progression. A further important reason is the placebo effect in the clinical trial. Using the placebo group as the basis for extrapolation will logically also project this effect forward. This example illustrates very well the importance of the datasets that are used to model diseases.

Figure 32 **Extrapolation of disease progression**

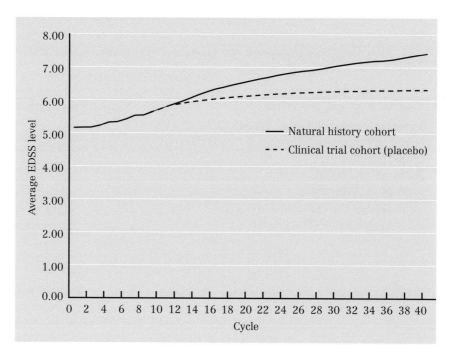

The latest version of the model combines the two types of MS for patients with active disease, based on the argument that costs and utilities are related to EDSS, and not different for different types of MS. The model uses two five-year trials with Betaferon for the first years, and the natural history data for extrapolation (Table 37). This increases the number of observations, making the model more reliable and allowing confidence intervals and acceptability curves to be estimated. In this model, the cost per QALY gained with Betaferon is SEK 66,200 and, as illustrated in Figure 33, the probability that the cost per QALY is less than SEK 500,000 for a patient starting in state 3 or 4 is 80%.

There are several issues that need to be mentioned here. The fact that the cost per QALY decreases with each version of the model could potentially lead to doubts about the process, in view of the current discussion about the benefit and the high cost of the new treatments. However, the results are only changed due to the addition of more reliable data or looking at different groups of patients, not to the modelling process. Such a situation is quite frequent, when research in a disease is very active.

Another issue is that treatment in the model is stopped at three (or five) years, which clearly is not realistic in clinical practice. However, the model incorporates no further benefit of treatment when it is stopped, but simply carries forward from the EDSS levels reached at that point. Outside an exacerbation, there is limited fluctuation in the EDSS scores as they express residual disability rather than a temporary treatment effect. The cost-

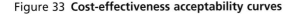

Figure 33 **Cost-effectiveness acceptability curves**

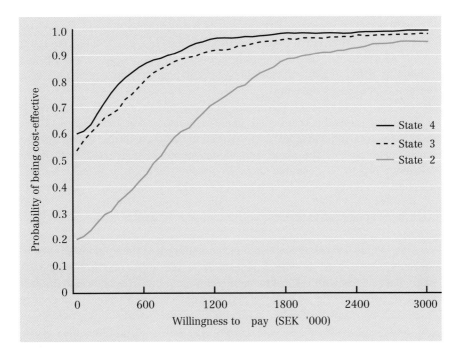

effectiveness ratio therefore really expresses what can be achieved with the treatment in terms of a lower EDSS score, for however long treatment is given, and carrying this effect forward appears acceptable. Continuing treatment in the model beyond the period for which clinical data are available would involve making assumptions about the clinical effect at each level of disability – which is not a very good solution. This is different from the Rheumatoid Arthritis example, where the disability measure is partly based on transient symptoms, and the effect achieved during the trial may therefore not carry over fully.

References

Kobelt G, Jönsson L, Henriksson F, Fredrikson S, Jönsson B (2000). Cost-utility of interferon beta-1b in secondary progressive multiple sclerosis. International Journal of Technology Assessment in Health Care 16(3):768-780.

Kobelt G, Jönsson L, Miltenburger C (2002). Cost-utility analysis of interferon beta-1b in secondary progressive multiple sclerosis using natural history disease data. International Journal of Technology Assessment in Health Care 18(1):127-138.

Kobelt G, Jönsson L, Fredriksson S, Jönsson B (2001). Cost-utility analysis of interferon ß-1b in the treatment of different types of multiple sclerosis. SSE/EFI Working Paper in Economics and Finance No. 459, August, Stockholm School of Economics, Stockholm.

3.7 Cost-benefit analysis

As mentioned in the previous chapter, it is frequently not possible to reduce the outcomes of alternative treatment programmes to a single effect common to both alternatives. Cost-utility analysis offers one approach to solving this problem by using quality-adjusted life years or healthy-year equivalents as a common effectiveness measure.

An alternative method is cost-benefit analysis (Johannesson and Jönsson, 1991) where both costs and outcomes are measured in monetary terms. With costs and benefits expressed in the same unit of measurement it is possible to judge whether a project is desirable (benefits greater than costs) from a societal viewpoint. In addition, cost-benefit analysis enables comparison of investments not only within the health care sector but also a comparison of the net benefits of investments in non-health sectors, such as education, with those in health care.

However, to date few cost-benefit studies for health care interventions have been published. One reason is ethical objections to placing a monetary value on health, particularly with respect to valuing a human life. This is despite the fact that there are numerous everyday examples where health is valued in monetary terms, such as compensation for death and disability, and public expenditure on road safety projects. A second reason is that cost-minimization, cost-effectiveness or cost-utility analyses will often yield sufficient data for decisions on resource allocation to be made, and cost-benefit analysis is not needed.

In a cost-benefit analysis a health care programme is considered good value for money when the value of the total benefit exceeds the total costs. Costs are ideally measured as opportunity costs, i.e. the best alternative benefit. Benefits are best measured by the maximum willingness to pay (WTP) for the outcomes of a project.

The theoretical base for cost-benefit analyses is economic welfare theory and the concept of consumer surplus, i.e. willingness to pay over and above the price actually paid, developed more than 50 years ago. The methods to measure health outcomes in monetary terms have however only recently been adapted. The standard method, **contingent valuation**, uses survey methods to measure people's WTP and was originally developed in the area of valuing environmental benefits, where it is still widely used.

3.7.1 Contingent valuation
Contingent valuation questions can be divided into open-ended and discrete questions. In an open-ended valuation the respondents are asked to state their maximum willingness to pay for the benefit, and the technique most used is the so-called bidding game. A bidding game resembles an auction, where a first bid is made to the respondent who either accepts or rejects. Depending on the answer, the bid is then lowered or increased until the respondent's maximum willingness to pay is reached.

In the alternative method, discrete questions of the yes/no or binary type are asked, which means that the respondent accepts or rejects the bid. Through varying the bid in different sub-samples it is possible to calculate the percentage of respondents who are willing to pay as a function of price (bid).

As with all methods used in economic evaluation to value the benefits, the contingent valuation method is better suited in some cases and not applicable in others. One situation where the technique has shown good results is where the health gains can be well defined and where the patients know exactly what they are paying for, such as avoiding asthma attacks, angina attacks or episodes of pain. In an area such as prevention, although this concerns risk decisions of the type that individuals have to make in everyday life, the health gains are much more difficult to describe, and probabilities of an event happening are usually small, which makes it harder for patients to respond. Currently, it appears that discrete binary questions are giving better results, as in the bidding game the influence of the starting bid can heavily influence the results (starting point bias).

For the contingent valuation method to provide valid estimates of willingness to pay, it has to be the case that willingness to pay increases with increasing size of the health gain. This is clearly shown in the following study examples. The absolute figures obtained should, however, be interpreted with great caution. Even if the individuals' willingness to pay is related to the explanatory variables in the hypothesized way, it is still possible that the estimated willingness to pay systematically underestimates or overestimates the individuals' true willingness to pay. To compare hypothetical and true willingness to pay for health changes is currently one of the important issues for research in this field.

Study Example 10 – *angina pectoris*

Willingness to pay studies are best suited to disease areas where a patient related benefit can be easily expressed as a single outcome measure. In a recent study in the cardiovascular field (Kartman et al., 1996), the contingent valuation method was used to assess individuals' willingness to pay for a treatment that would reduce the number of angina attacks.

Angina pectoris is a widespread cardiovascular disease that has been characterised as chest pain associated with transient episodes of myocardial ischaemia resulting from an imbalance between oxygen supply and tissue demand. There is no clear consensus on whether to speak about pain or discomfort during attack, but the frequency of attacks can be used to measure the severity of the disease.

The question put to 400 Swedish patients with angina pectoris was as follows: "Imagine that there are two treatments for your disease. The first is your current treatment, the second is more effective and has been shown to reduce weekly attacks by 50%. However, for each three-month period of the second treatment you have to pay a certain amount from your own income." (The percentage reduction was varied to 25% and 75% in randomised subsamples).

Table 38 **Mean willingness to pay for different rates of reduction of angina attacks (SEK, 1994 prices)**

Method	Attack rate reduction		
	25%	50%	75%
Binary question data	1,873	2,499	2,692
Bidding game data	1,388	2,079	3,350

Source: Kartman et al. (1996)

The study used both the binary question and the bidding game techniques. The main problem with the bidding game approach is that the reported willingness to pay is likely to be affected by the size of the first bid offered, a phenomenon called starting point bias. With binary questions, each respondent only accepts or rejects one bid, and the bid is varied in different subsamples to determine the mean willingness to pay for the good.

The answers were analysed with multiple regression analysis that also included a set of explanatory variables capturing angina status, weekly attack rate and income levels of the respondents. It was hypothesized that the willingness to pay would rise with increasing severity of angina and an increasing weekly attack rate. Results are shown in Table 38.

Figure 34 **Proportion of Individuals Willing to Pay as a Function of the Amount (in SEK) (pooled data for all attack rate reductions)**

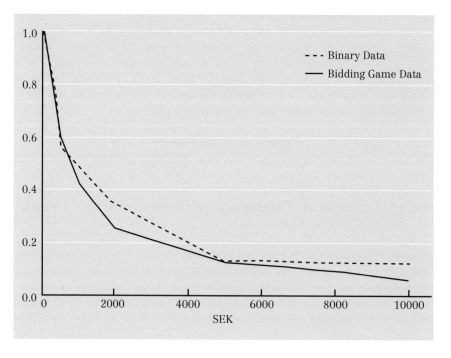

Figure 34 shows the proportion of individuals willing to pay as a function of the bid for both the binary and the bidding game data.

Reference

Kartman B, Andersson F, Johannesson M (1996). Willingness to pay for reductions in angina pectoris attacks. Medical Decision Making 16(3):248-53.

Study example 11 – *incontinence*

A very similar study investigated the willingness to pay (WTP) for a reduction in symptoms of urge incontinence, a disease where the outcome is somewhat more difficult to express as one single patient-related benefit (Johannesson et al., 1997). Patients with urge incontinence experience symptoms of urgency, urinary frequency and involuntary loss of urine. Quality of life is impaired, as urgency is often associated with colic-like pain, and daytime urinary frequency can severely limit activities while nocturnal frequency can be associated with persistent fatigue. Treatments include physiotherapy, pharmacological treatment and, in rare cases, surgery. Drug therapy at the time of this study was hampered by limited efficacy or severe side effects leading to extremely poor compliance. In the absence of cure or effective treatment, sanitary protections are widely used.

Table 39 Quality of life of patients with urge incontinence and correlations between quality of life and severity of symptoms

	Urge incontinence	*Matched normals*		*Correlation coefficient*	
	Mean (SD)	*Mean (SD)*	*P*	*(Symptom score and QoL)*	*P*
SF-36					
Physical functioning	66.0 (25.2)	75.3 (11.8)	< 0.001	–0.22	<0.001
Role, physical	55.3 (43.0)	70.2 (14.1)	< 0.001	–0.16	<0.001
Bodily pain	55.9 (26.9)	67.8 (4.8)	< 0.001	–0.14	0.004
General health	56.3 (24.4)	67.7 (7.5)	< 0.001	–0.23	<0.001
Vitality	53.7 (26.3)	64.6 (7.1)	< 0.001	–0.19	<0.001
Social functioning	75.8 (26.0)	85.0 (4.6)	< 0.001	–0.23	<0.001
Role, emotional	67.0 (40.9)	78.4 (9.4)	< 0.001	–0.10	0.044
Mental health	70.5 (22.9)	78.3 (3.7)	< 0.001	–0.17	0.001
EuroQol					
EQ-5D	0.68	0.80	< 0.0001	–0.25	<0.001
Rating scale	65.56	79.0	< 0.0001	–0.20	<0.001

Table 40 **Mean and median willingness to pay for a reduction in incontinence symptoms**

Reduction in the frequency of micturitions and episodes of incontinence		
	25%	*50%*
Median WTP	240 SEK	466 SEK
Mean WTP	529 SEK	1027 SEK

Frequency of micturitions and episodes of involuntary urine loss are not independent, as patients cope by frequent visits to the bathroom to avoid episodes of leakage. Clinical trials will measure both symptoms separately, but for a WTP questionnaire it is important to express the outcome with one measure. This study investigated the possibility of combining these symptoms into one outcome measure and tested the appropriateness of the measure by assessing its correlation with health related quality of life.

A specific WTP questionnaire, as well as the EQ-5D and the SF-36, was mailed to a sample of patients. The WTP question was in binary format; patients were asked whether they would pay a given price for a given reduction in symptoms. The percentage reduction in symptoms was varied between 25% and 50%, and six price levels were used. (The range of prices, as well as the understanding of the question, had been pre-tested.)

The combined outcome measure correlated significantly with all domains of the SF-36, as well as with utilities, as can be seen in Table 39, and was therefore considered acceptable. Patients were willing to pay more for the larger percentage reduction in symptoms, which is one factor by which the understanding of the WTP question can be judged (Table 40 and Figure 35). WTP increased as the severity of the symptoms increased (and thus the potential absolute benefit), and also with higher income, as expected (Table 41). Overall, this study is a very clear example of a WTP study where all parameters "behaved" as they should.

Table 41 **Sensitivity analysis: median and mean WTP (SEK) for a 25% reduction in symptoms at different levels of symptom severity and income**

Monthly income (SEK)	Median (mean) willingness to pay in SEK for different levels of symptom severity		
	15	*20*	*25*
5000	134 (294)	168 (409)	234 (515)
10000	273 (601)	378 (832)	476 (1047)
15000	379 (834)	525 (1155)	661 (1545)

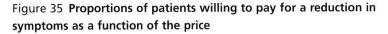

Figure 35 **Proportions of patients willing to pay for a reduction in symptoms as a function of the price**

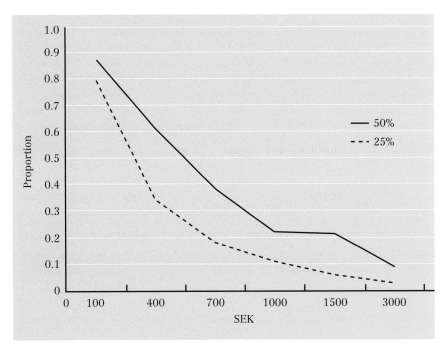

Reference

Johannesson M, O'Conor R M, Kobelt G, Mattiasson A (1997). Willingness to pay for reduced incontinence symptoms. British Journal of Urology 80:557-562.

Summary of cost-benefit analysis:

- **In a cost-benefit analysis both the costs and the benefits are calculated in monetary terms.**

- **The results are expressed as one figure, representing the difference between the benefits and the costs (B - C).**

- **Contingent valuation is one method of assessing an individual's willingness to pay for health gains.**

- **Cost-benefit analysis allows comparison of investment decisions in the health care sector with investment decisions in other parts of the economy.**

4 Guidelines for Economic Evaluation

As discussed in Section 1.2, a number of countries around the world have, in the last decade, formally incorporated an economic criterion into the decision making process in health care, principally as a means of assessing whether or not a new pharmaceutical should be listed on a publicly reimbursed formulary. Each of these initiatives has been accompanied by the development of guidelines designed specifically to support the particular policy requirement, with the exception of British Columbia, where submissions can follow the Ontario or Canadian Coordinating Office for Health Technology Assessment (CCOHTA) guidelines.

The CCOHTA (1997) document may be seen as a generic set of guidelines for those undertaking economic evaluations and, despite the title 'Guidelines for economic evaluation of pharmaceuticals: Canada', is intended to be applicable to any health technology. The summary of guideline statements is reproduced in Box 10. A more context specific set of guidelines, namely the guidance for manufacturers and sponsors in making submissions to the UK's National Institute for Clinical Excellence (NICE), is summarised in Box 11.

The fact that NICE's guidance, unlike the CCOHTA document, was developed to support a particular programme of technology appraisals, is reflected in some of the specific methods recommended. For example, the NICE guidance notes that the target audience for the analysis is the NHS and Personal Social Services (PSS) decision maker, and that issues concerning the generalisability of data to the context of the NHS in England and Wales (to which NICE's recommendations apply) should be considered. Where cost utility analysis is undertaken, health state preferences of this population (England and Wales) are the most relevant for NICE submissions. In comparison, the CCOHTA guidelines recommend simply that the preferences of the public should be used and suggest that since the Quality of Well-being Scale (QWB), the Health Utilities Index (HUI) and the EuroQol EQ-5D all meet this criterion, any one is suitable.

Substantive points of methodology on which the two documents disagree are the appropriate perspective for the analysis, the type of economic evaluation and the relevant approach to discounting. In accordance with the methodological literature generally, the CCOHTA guidelines strongly recommend that the societal perspective be adopted and, while advising that results be presented from other viewpoints, including that of the primary decision maker, view all costs as relevant no matter who incurs them. These would include costs falling on sectors of the economy outside health care, such as education, those borne by the patient and family and, where appropriate, time costs (which include indirect or productivity costs). The NICE guidance, on the other hand, focuses primarily on NHS and PSS costs, putting far less emphasis on patients' out-of-pocket expenses, the cost of their time undergoing treatment or the impact on productivity.

As far as the type of economic evaluation is concerned, the NICE guidance recommends the use of cost-effectiveness or cost-utility analysis, whereas the CCOHTA guidelines take a broader view of the type of analysis admissible but express a preference for cost-utility analysis (CUA) or cost-benefit analysis (CBA). In contrast to the equal footing given to CUA and CBA by CCOHTA, NICE emphasizes the importance of morbidity and mortality as outcomes which form the basis of CUA but neglects the methods available to value those outcomes in monetary terms.

The third point of disagreement considered here reflects the divergence of the NICE guidance from many other sets of guidelines in terms of how future flows of costs and benefits are to be treated. The CCOHTA guidelines adopt the majority view that both costs and health effects should be discounted at the same rate, but that a zero discounting option should form one of the sensitivity analyses. The impact of differential discount rates is to be treated as supplementary information. NICE, in contrast, adopts the position of the Department of Health and National Assembly of Wales (based on a UK Treasury recommendation) that a lower rate of discount be used for health effects (1.5%) than for costs (6%). Options to be explored in sensitivity analyses include maintaining this rate on costs, but with the same rate (6%) and with a zero rate for effects.

While it is possible to emphasis disagreements between the methods advocated by CCOHTA and NICE, the latter were developed partly with the aid of a review of other guidelines, including those produced by CCOHTA. There are, therefore, large areas of common ground between the methods proposed by the two organizations. Both concentrate on the need to generate effectiveness data, rather than relying on efficacy measures, and recognize the importance of modelling techniques to translate one into the other. Both focus on existing practice/most frequently used alternative as the relevant comparator, although the CCOHTA guidelines also specify that 'minimum practice' be included (in a NICE submission, comparators for the analysis are determined by an initial scoping exercise). Each body regards sub-group analyses as admissible, with the proviso that they should be based on prior reasoning. Both sets of recommendations prompt analysts to allow for equity concerns by identifying those groups of patients who would be most likely to benefit from the intervention being evaluated. Various other points of consensus could be discussed; indeed, if this comparison were to be repeated across a variety of guidelines developed by different countries, it is likely that a core set of agreed methodological principles would emerge, but with individual countries making adjustments where appropriate to suit their own particular requirements.

Box 10 **CCOHTA guidelines (1997)**

I. SUMMARY OF GUIDELINE STATEMENTS

Guideline 1. Target Audience
The primary target audience (decision-maker) for the study must be identified. Secondary target audiences (if applicable) should also be listed.

Guideline 2. Timing of Studies
Pharmacoeconomic studies can be undertaken at any point in a product's life cycle. Suggestions are given on the timing of studies and on the types of decision-making situations which call for the presentation of economic evidence.

Guideline 3. Management of Studies
There are no restrictions on who can do studies. All studies should, however, be consistent with these Guidelines.

Guideline 4. Incremental and Total Analysis
Costs and effects must be reported as increments (that is, as differences between two alternatives) and as totals. Increments must be used in the pharmacoeconomic evaluation.

Guideline 5. Analytic Technique
If all consequences are essentially identical between the drug and the relevant comparators, a cost-minimization analysis (CMA) is adequate. In other instances, a cost-consequence analysis (CCA) is required plus one or more of the following: cost-effectiveness analysis (CEA), cost-utility analysis (CUA), and cost-benefit analysis (CBA). Consistent with the desire to permit broad comparisons, CUA or CBA are preferred. Researchers should present the data using a variety of techniques, to maximize the information content and to contribute to the development of these methodologies.

Guideline 6. Indications
The study must clearly specify the target population for the drug. Any investigations of patient subgroups, disease subtypes, severity levels, comorbidity groups, etc., should be clearly identified by an explicit hypothesis in the study protocol. Economic evaluation should be performed overall and, data permitting, for those subgroups that were identified in the protocol for their possible differential effectiveness, costs and/or preferences.

Guideline 7. Treatment Comparator
The drug treatment should be compared with both existing practice and minimum practice. The relevant comparators may be other drugs, other medical care such as surgery, or even no treatment. Existing practice would either be the single most prevalent clinical practice (if there is one that is

dominant), or it could be current practice weighted by market share. Minimum practice would normally be either the lowest cost comparator that is more effective than placebo, or the do-nothing alternative, as appropriate. In addition to these two formal comparators, all other reasonable alternative therapies should be at least discussed in the report.

Guideline 8. Perspective
All studies should report from a comprehensive societal perspective. That perspective should be transparently broken down into those of other relevant viewpoints, including that of the primary decision-maker. A financial impact analysis from the viewpoint of the primary decision-maker may also be undertaken, if requested, but technically is a budgeting exercise and does not constitute part of the economic evaluation.

Guideline 9. Analytic Horizon
Every effort should be made to extend the analytic horizon to capture all relevant outcomes. When modelled data are needed to meet this requirement, the structure and rationale of the model must be presented.

Guideline 10. Assumptions
A comprehensive listing of assumptions and associated rationale must be contained within the explanation of the methodology for the analysis.

Guideline 11. Efficacy versus Effectiveness
Ideally, pharmacoeconomic studies should report on drug effectiveness rather than efficacy. Because effectiveness data are generally not available, appropriate modelling techniques based on sound pharmacoepidemiology (e.g. using epidemiologic studies to estimate patient compliance with therapy in the real world) are permissible. All assumptions used in such extrapolation techniques must be stated explicitly and thoroughly tested with sensitivity analysis.

Guideline 12. Health-Related Quality of Life (HRQOL)
If HRQOL is being included in a prospective study as an outcome, it is normally advisable to include, where possible and feasible, one instrument from each of the following three types: specific measures, generic profiles, and preference-based measures. Any drug product that demonstrates improved effectiveness over its comparator(s) and impacts on a patient's HRQOL should probably be evaluated for this outcome using these tools.

Guideline 13. Outcomes for Cost-Utility Analysis
Both quantity of life (survival) and HRQOL results should be reported separately, and the method of combining the two described in a transparent manner. The current recommended method for the primary analysis is to combine quantity and quality of life using quality-adjusted life years (QALYs). Alternatives, such as disability-adjusted life years (DALYs), healthy years

equivalents (HYEs) or saved young life equivalents (SAVEs) may be useful as secondary analyses in some studies. To be suitable for use as quality weights for calculating quality-adjusted life years, scores must be based on preferences and measured on an interval scale where dead has a score of 0 and healthy has a score of 1.

Direct preference measurements can be undertaken with various instruments. Analysts should select an instrument that suits the problem, and should justify their selection. Alternatively, preferences can be determined indirectly using one of the major systems available. Here again, analysts should select a system that suits the problem, and should justify their selection.

Guideline 14. Outcomes for Cost-Benefit Analysis
The human capital approach (HCA) to assigning values to outcomes in CBA is incomplete because it focuses primarily on lost work time. If this approach is used, measures taken to overcome these shortcomings should be clearly described.

While realizing the incomplete and experimental nature of this method, theoretically, the preferred approach to the assignment of values to outcomes in CBA is contingent valuation as a means of eliciting an assessment of willingness to pay (WTP). If this approach is used, the investigator(s) should be explicit with regards to the assumptions and methods utilized. In addition, the measures taken to reduce bias and an outline of the scope tests carried out to determine validity should be clearly described.

Guideline 15. Source of Preferences
The appropriate source of preferences depends on the use of the analysis and the viewpoint. For provincial drug plans, which are tax supported, the appropriate viewpoint is societal and the appropriate source of preferences for outcomes is the informed general public. The three major systems for the indirect determination of preferences (QWB, HUI, EQ-5D) are all scored based on preferences from the general public and, so, are suitable.

Analysts who wish to measure preferences directly should ideally do so on the general public, suitably informed. Patients in a study may, however, be a reasonable proxy for the informed general public, especially when they are providing preferences for hypothetical states. Preferences should be based on scientifically sound measurements. Investigators undertaking direct measurements of preferences must justify their source of subjects, and describe the exact population from which the preferences were derived and the precise methods of measurement.

Guideline 16. Equity
All equity assumptions, whether implicit or explicit, must be highlighted in any analysis intended for use in the resource allocation process. Results should be

presented using equal weights for all lives, life years or QALYs, but the presentation should be sufficiently transparent to make it feasible for decision-makers to substitute different weights. Analysts should identify which groups of individuals would be the main beneficiaries if the programme were implemented.

Guideline 17. Discounting Future Outcomes

Future outcomes should be discounted at the same rate as costs. The base case discount rate is 5% per year. This rate must be varied in a sensitivity analysis, with a discount rate of 0% (no discounting) at minimum. Analysts should also consider using a 3% rate for comparability with future studies. When it is believed the analysis should differentiate between discount rates for outcomes and costs, these results should be presented as a supplementary analysis and the relevance fully explained.

Guideline 18. Cost Identification

A probability tree of the therapeutic pathway which describes all relevant downstream events should be provided, when appropriate. From the societal viewpoint, cost items that should be included are all direct health care costs, social services costs, spillover costs on other sectors such as education, and costs that fall on the patient and family. Cost items that should be excluded are those not relevant to the therapeutic pathway such as those not related to the treatment being evaluated, costs relevant only to the clinical trial, and transfer payments such as sickness pay, unemployment insurance and welfare payments.

When relevant, lost time should be documented and reported as part of the description of the impact of the intervention. If HRQOL is an outcome measure in the study, some lost time will likely contribute to changes in HRQOL. Depending on the viewpoint, some lost time will represent a real cost in terms of lost resources and should be included as a cost item, but should also be tested with sensitivity analysis.

Guideline 19. Cost Measurement (Resources Used)

Resources used in treatment must first be described in natural (non-dollar) units. All resource utilization data derived from international trials must be validated for Canadian practice.

Guideline 20. Cost Valuation (Unit Prices)

Economic definitions of costs must be used and the concept of opportunity cost recognized. Investigators performing analyses in the Canadian setting should refer to the CCOHTA *Guidance Document for the Costing Process* for further direction regarding costing issues.

Guideline 21. Discounting Future Costs

As with future outcomes, all studies must discount future costs at an initial rate of 5% per year in the base case. This rate must be varied in a sensitivity analysis, with a discount rate of 0% (no discounting) at minimum. Analysts should also consider using a 3% rate for comparability with future studies. If differential discount rates are to be used for outcomes and costs, then the results should be presented as a supplementary analysis and the relevance fully explained.

Guideline 22. Dealing with Uncertainty
All studies must clearly address the issue of uncertainty (whether it arises from sampling error or from assumptions) and justify the methods used. Sampling errors can be dealt with by making use of confidence intervals. In addition, for each important assumption, alternative plausible assumptions must be included. Investigators are encouraged to use approaches such as Monte Carlo simulation, which varies all factors simultaneously.

Guideline 23. Reporting Results
All results must be reported in disaggregated detail first, with aggregations and the use of value judgements (e.g. preference scores) being introduced into the presentation as late as possible. A probability tree of clinical outcomes should be provided for the relevant alternatives. Detailed technical reports, with patient confidentiality protected, should be made available to decision-makers. Reports should either follow the standardized reporting structure or be linked to it.

Guideline 24. Portability of Economic Evaluations
The portability of an economic evaluation is an issue which should be considered during the development of the study, as well as during the interpretation and dissemination of study results. Consideration must be given to two aspects of the applicability of the analysis to the local setting. The first aspect is the distinction between efficacy and effectiveness. The second aspect is the validity of transferring results (i.e. economic, clinical and humanistic) from one country or health care jurisdiction to another. These considerations are especially important when working in the context of multinational, multi-centre trials.

Guideline 25. Disclosure of Relationships
Funding and reporting relationships must be clearly described. The investigators must have independence regarding methodological considerations at all stages of the study, and must have the right of publication in the journal of their choice.

Box 11 **UK NICE Guidance for Manufacturers and Sponsors (2001)**

SUMMARY OF GUIDANCE

2.3   Specific Guidance

2.3.1 Perspective

The evaluation should be conducted from the perspective of the NHS and Personal Social Service (PSS) decision-maker.   That is to say the benefits should include all clinical and health-related benefits valued from the perspective of society, and costing should include all use of NHS and PSS resources required to achieve those benefits.

2.4   Context of the Evaluation

2.4.1 Problem Definition

The nature and scope of the problem addressed in any evaluation should be clearly defined and with reference to the Institute's scope for the appraisal. This should include the clinical problem, the patient group being treated (e.g. age and sex distribution and co-morbidities), the comparators being evaluated and the treatment context (e.g. hospital, clinic, community).   Manufacturers and sponsors should provide background information on the clinical problem to which their technology offers a solution.   This should include estimates of patient numbers (incidence and prevalence) and recent trends in these figures.

2.4.2 Development of the Technology

The development status of the technology, including the history of its development, the current range of applications and potential future uses, should be described.

2.4.3 Forms of Analysis

The analysis should take the form of a cost-effectiveness analysis or cost-utility analysis depending on the nature of the clinical problem being addressed.

2.4.4 Time Horizon

The time span of the analysis should cover the period over which the main health effects and health care resource use are expected to be experienced. This may require extrapolation beyond the period for which data from controlled clinical trials are available. The nature of any modelling used in the extrapolation should be fully explained and the sensitivity of the results to the method of extrapolation and the choice of time horizon should be thoroughly tested.

2.5   Comparisons

The choice of comparator will usually be determined by the scope for the appraisal by the Institute in its request for submissions. The main comparator should normally be the most frequently used intervention for the patient group in question.

2.6   Outcome Measurement

The preferred form of outcome data for evaluation of health care technologies is long-term clinical effectiveness (morbidity and mortality) with self-assessment of health status by patients at each distinct stage of disease progression. This facilitates cost-effectiveness analysis and, when combined with data on social preferences between health states, can be used in cost-utility analysis. Modelling techniques may be used to adjust efficacy data to reflect what is expected in practice. The scientific basis of any modelling must be justified and the assumptions, data and processes made transparent and subjected to sensitivity analysis.

2.7   Generalisability of Study Results

The settings, populations and methods by which outcomes and costs are measured in the original studies from which data are drawn should be described and the implications of generalising the data to the NHS in England and Wales explained.

2.8   Presentation of Clinical Data

2.8.1   Reporting of Results
The clear presentation of clinical trial data is important and the Institute recommends that manufacturers and sponsors should refer to published guides including the International Committee on Harmonisation (ICH) Guidelines.

2.8.2   Format of Reporting
The results for the principal outcomes of each study included in submissions should be reported individually, preferably in tabular form. Numerators and denominators of rates (and proportions) should be provided. Estimates should be expressed as appropriate central estimates with suitable interval assessments.

Graphical presentation should be used where it substantially assists in interpretation of the results. The relevant underlying data should be presented, if necessary in an appendix to the submission.

2.8.3   Risk Estimates
Results should be reported both as relative estimates and absolute estimates. The period over which the risk estimates have been calculated should be stated and these estimates should generally be annualised.

2.8.4   Sub-Group Analysis
Sub-group analysis is justified where there is a sound biological a priori rationale for doing so (e.g. 'high risk' patients) and where there is evidence that clinical effectiveness or cost-effectiveness may vary between such groups.

2.8.5   Interpretation of Results
Manufacturers and sponsors of technologies should include the data on the

clinical effectiveness of their product within a systematic review of evidence of the effectiveness of their product in the relevant patient group.

2.9 Valuation of outcomes

2.9.1 Utilities
When cost-utility analysis is undertaken the valuation of health gain must reflect the health state preferences indicated by the analytical perspectives. Given the perspective of the Institute (Section 2.3.1) the most relevant values are those of the general population of England and Wales.

2.9.2 Productivity
Impacts on social productivity may be assessed if considered sufficiently important in specific cases. The methods used to measure and value the productivity gains should be fully presented.

2.10 Resource Use and Costs

2.10.1 Resource Use Identification
The principal component of resource use from the Institute's perspective is direct provision of health and social care in association with the use of the technology. Models extrapolating the long-term outcomes of treatment from short-term clinical trials should include future health care resources consumed in managing the long-term sequelae of the disease under study (e.g. myocardial infarction after re-stenosis post-PTCA) but not those used for the treatment of unrelated conditions. Resources used by patients in obtaining treatment (e.g. time and travel) should be recorded separately.

2.10.2 Resource Measurement
The resources used by each treatment approach must be presented separately, aggregated in natural units such as hospital days, number of consultations and volumes of drugs. The sources of the resource data must be clearly stated.

2.10.3 Resource Costing
Total costs for each comparator should be calculated by applying standard unit values to the quantities of each type of resource. These unit costs should generally reflect the average cost of the resource to the NHS and PSS. The source of each unit cost should be cited.

2.11 Discounting

Future outcomes and costs must be discounted to reflect social time preferences and social opportunity costs of resources. The conventional view is that benefits and costs should be discounted at the same rate. The current recommendation of the DH and the NAW is that costs should be discounted at 6% per annum and benefits at $1^1/2$%. To maintain consistency with appraisals undertaken elsewhere within the NHS these values should be used in the base case analysis of evaluations in submissions to the Institute. Sensitivity analyses should also be carried out using, amongst others, the combinations 6% costs and 6% for outcomes, and 6% for costs and 0% outcomes.

2.12   Presentation of Results

2.12.1 Incremental Comparisons
Incremental cost-effectiveness ratios and/or cost-utility ratios should be presented, as well as total costs and outcomes for each comparator.

2.12.2
The results should also be presented in disaggregated form so that the nature and extent of differences between comparators are easily discernable. For example, mortality and quality of life data should be presented separately as well as in the form of utility measures such as QALYs.

2.12.3
Quantities of resources used and unit costs for each type of resource should be presented separately.

2.12.4 Uncertainty
Wherever possible the results of the economic comparisons should be subjected to sensitivity analysis testing. For example, when data are drawn exclusively from clinical trials, 95% confidence intervals can be calculated for cost-effectiveness ratios. When data are drawn from a variety of sources and used in a modelling framework, probabilistic sensitivity analysis is recommended in order to take account of the uncertainty around data values. Bayesian approaches which reflect effects of uncertainty would be acceptable, provided they are transparent.

2.13   Wider NHS Impact

2.13.1 Budget Impact
Manufacturers and sponsors should provide an analysis of the likely budget impact on the NHS of the use of their technology. For new technologies, this should include estimates of the changing budget impact over a 3 to 5 year period as a result of varying diffusion rates and also an estimate of impact once diffusion has reached a 'steady state'.

2.13.2 Service Impact
When a technology has requirements for specific health care resources, for example, specialist training for clinical personnel or availability of particular diagnostic services, these should be explained in general terms.

2.14   Equity

Manufacturers and sponsors should provide as much detail as possible on the probable clinical and social status of patients likely to benefit from the use of their technology. They should also provide information on any aspects of the technology which might lead to increased or reduced personal costs to patients and their carers and families.

5 Conclusion

Health economics applies the theories, tools and concepts of economics to the topic of health and health care. Health economics is now a central tool of health policy makers' attempts to introduce more efficiency into health care organisation, financing and resource allocation. Policy makers, payers, providers and patients are all involved.

Economic evaluations analyse the consequences of using new or established therapies, in terms of both their benefits and their costs, compared to alternatives. They provide part of the basis on which policy makers can make resource allocation decisions in an environment of finite budgets.

The methodology to be used in economic evaluations, while still evolving, has been defined according to the state of the art by guidelines for pharmacoeconomic studies in some countries, and in general by academic publications on good methodological principles. As illustrated by the Australian Pharmaceutical Benefits Advisory Committee's guidelines, now in their third generation, such guidelines and other discussions of methodological principles (such as this book) should be seen as work in progress. It is worth considering, therefore, the issues that may attract greater attention over time when recommendations for the conduct of economic evaluation are debated.

The examples in this book have focused largely on the use of modelling techniques which synthesise data from a number of sources to derive estimates of cost-effectiveness. They have also concentrated on the economic evaluation of pharmaceuticals, the technology towards which most policy attention with regard to the use of an economic criterion has been directed. These modelling techniques are widely accepted and used and are likely to remain so, particularly in the context of pharmaceutical companies making submissions to reimbursement authorities at a time when little clinical trial evidence may be available.

As studies based on modelling become presented increasingly as tools to help make decisions and as they come under scrutiny from a wider range of decision making bodies, the issue of study quality is likely to acquire greater significance. Although the means of assessing quality have become more sophisticated, as the BMJ guidelines (Drummond and Jefferson, 1996) in Table 42 illustrate, a checklist approach may be inadequate to the task of undertaking a critical appraisal of economic evaluations. Guidance on assessing quality may need to become more specific to different types of study or particular aspects of studies, perhaps along the lines of the approach proposed by Sculpher et al. (2000) for decision analytic models.

In addition to generating cost-effectiveness estimates for making decisions about the relative values of different treatments, modelling approaches could

Table 42 BMJ referees' checklist (also to be used, implicitly, by authors)

Item	Yes	No	Not clear	Not appropriate
Study design				
1 The research question is stated	☐	☐	☐	
2 The economic importance of the research question is stated	☐	☐	☐	
3 The viewpoint(s) of the analysis are clearly stated and justified	☐	☐	☐	
4 The rationale for choosing the alternative programmes or interventions compared is stated	☐	☐	☐	
5 The alternatives being compared are clearly described	☐	☐	☐	
6 The form of economic evaluation used is stated	☐	☐	☐	
7 The choice of form of economic evaluation is justified in relation to the questions addressed	☐	☐	☐	
Data Collection				
8 The source(s) of effectiveness estimates used are stated	☐	☐	☐	
9 Details of the design and results of effectiveness study are given (if based on a single study)	☐	☐	☐	☐
10 Details of the method of synthesis or meta-analysis of estimates are given (if based on an overview of a number of effectiveness studies)	☐	☐	☐	☐
11 The primary outcome measure(s) for the economic evaluation are clearly stated	☐	☐	☐	
12 Methods to value health states and other benefits are stated	☐	☐	☐	☐
13 Details of the subjects from whom valuations were obtained are given	☐	☐	☐	☐
14 Productivity changes (if included) are reported separately	☐	☐	☐	☐
15 The relevance of productivity changes to the study question is discussed	☐	☐	☐	☐

Item	Yes	No	Not clear	Not appropriate
Study design				
16 Quantities of resources are reported separately from their unit costs	☐	☐	☐	
17 Methods for the estimation of quantities and unit costs are described	☐	☐	☐	
18 Currency and price data are recorded	☐	☐	☐	
19 Details of currency of price adjustments for inflation or currency conversion are given	☐	☐	☐	
20 Details of any model used are given	☐	☐	☐	☐
21 The choice of model used and the key parameters on which it is based are justified	☐	☐	☐	☐
Analysis and interpretation of results				
22 Time horizon of costs and benefits is stated	☐	☐	☐	
23 The discount rate(s) is stated	☐	☐	☐	☐
24 The choice of rate(s) is justified	☐	☐	☐	☐
25 An explanation is given if costs or benefits are not discounted	☐	☐	☐	☐
26 Details of statistical tests and confidence intervals are given for stochastic data	☐	☐	☐	☐
27 The approach to sensitivity analysis is given	☐	☐	☐	☐
28 The choice of variables for sensitivity analysis is justified	☐	☐	☐	☐
29 The ranges over which the variables are varied are stated	☐	☐	☐	☐
30 Relevant alternatives are compared	☐	☐	☐	
31 Incremental analysis is reported	☐	☐	☐	☐
32 Major outcomes are presented in a disaggregated as well as aggregated form	☐	☐	☐	
33 The answer to the study question is given	☐	☐	☐	

Item	Yes	No	Not clear	Not appropriate
34 Conclusions follow from the data reported	☐	☐	☐	
35 Conclusions are accompanied by the appropriate caveats	☐	☐	☐	

be exploited by decision makers, perhaps at earlier stages of drug development, to help identify where further research is most useful. The potential of the value of information framework to assist in this endeavour has been illustrated by Claxton (1999). This approach is firmly rooted in a Bayesian view of decision making, where the decision maker is interested in the likelihood of an intervention being cost-effective, rather than whether the results of the analysis are statistically significant in the conventional sense.

It is not only a Bayesian interpretation of the uncertainty around a central estimate of the cost-effectiveness estimate that has appealed to analysts; there are also examples of full-blown Bayesian methods applied to economic analyses conducted alongside clinical trials. This is one aspect of economic evaluation which is likely to receive greater prominence in the coming years, as will issues like the estimation of cost-effectiveness according to different sub-groups, dealing with censored and missing cost (and outcome) data and the generalisability of study findings to other contexts.

These are among the points of methodology where advances can be expected to be welcomed by those actively engaged in conducting trial-based evaluations. However, from whatever direction refinements to the techniques of economic analysis are made, they will find a ready audience not only among practitioners but also in the policy making community as it searches for greater value for money in health care.

6 Bibliography

Al M J, van Hout B A (2000). A Bayesian approach to economic analyses of clinical trials: the case of stenting versus balloon angioplasty. Health Economics 9: 599-609.

Anis A H, Gagnon Y (2000). Using economic evaluations to make formulary coverage decisions: so much for guidelines. PharmacoEconomics 18(1):55-62.

Arikian S, Einarson T, Kobelt-Nguyen G, Schubert F (1994). A multinational pharmacoeconomic analysis of oral therapies for onychomycosis. British Journal of Dermatology 130 (Suppl43):35-44.

Briggs A H (2001). A Bayesian approach to stochastic cost-effectiveness analysis: an illustration and application to blood pressure control in type 2 diabetes. International Journal of Technology Assessment in Health Care 17(1): 69-82.

Briggs A H (2000). Handling uncertainty in cost-effectiveness models. PharmacoEconomics 17(5): 479-500.

Briggs A H, Wonderling D E, Mooney C Z (1997). Pulling cost-effectiveness analysis up by its bootstraps: a non-parametric approach to confidence interval estimation. Health Economics 6: 327-340.

Buxton M J, Drummond M F, van Hout B A, Prince R L, Sheldon T A, Szucs T, Vray M (1997). Modelling in economic evaluation: an unavoidable fact of life. Health Economics 6(3):217-27.

Canadian Coordinating Office for Health Technology Assessment (1997). Guidelines for economic evaluation of pharmaceuticals: Canada. 2nd ed. Ottawa: Canadian Coordinating Office for Health Technology Assessment (CCOHTA).

Claxton K (1999). The irrelevance of inference: a decision-making approach to the stochastic evaluation of health care technologies. Journal of Health Economics 18:341-364.

Cleland J, Takala A, Apajasalo M, Zethraeus N, Kobelt G (2001). Cost-effectiveness of levosimendan in severe low-output heart failure compared to dobutamine based on an international clinical trial (LIDO). Abstract, ISPOR (Cannes, France), November.

Commonwealth of Australia (1995). Guidelines for the pharmaceutical industry on preparation of submissions to the Pharmaceutical Benefits Advisory Committee: including submissions involving economic analyses. Canberra: Australian Government Printing Office.

Department of Health (1999). "Faster Access to Modern Treatment": How NICE Appraisal Will Work – A discussion paper. Leeds: NHS Executive.

Department of Health/ABPI (1994). UK guidance on good practice in the conduct of economic evaluations of medicines. British Journal of Medical Economics 7:63-64.

Dolan P, Gudex C, Kind P, Williams A (1995). A social tariff for EuroQol: results from a UK general population survey. Discussion Paper 138. York: University of York Centre for Health Economics.

Drummond M, Dubois D, Garattini L, Horisberger B, Jönsson B, Kristiansen I S, Le Pen C, Pinto C G, Poulsen P B, Rovira J, Rutten F, von der Schulenburg M G, Sintonen H (1999). Current Trends in the Use of Pharmacoeconomics and Outcomes Research in Europe. Value In Health 2(5):323-332.

Drummond M F, Jefferson T O (1996). Guidelines for authors and peer reviewers of economic submissions to the BMJ. BMJ 313: 275-283.

Drummond M, Mason J, Torrance G (1993). Some guidelines on the use of cost-effectiveness league tables. British Medical Journal 306(6877):570-2.

Drummond M, Rutten F, Brenna A, Pinto C G, Horisberger B, Jönsson B, Le Pen C, Rovira J, von der Schulenburg M G, Sintonen H, Torfs K (1993). Economic evaluation of pharmaceuticals: a European perspective. PharmacoEconomics 4(3):173-86.

Fieller E C (1954). Some problems in interval estimation with discussion. Journal of the Royal Statistical Society, Series B 16:75-188.

George B, Harris A, Mitchell A (2001). Cost-effectiveness analysis and the consistency of decision making: evidence from pharmaceutical reimbursement in Australia (1991 to 1996). PharmacoEconomics 19(11):1103-1109.

Gold M R, Siegel J E, Russell L B, Weinstein M C (1996) (eds). Cost-Effectiveness in Health and Medicine. New York: Oxford University Press.

Graf von der Schulenburg J-M (2000) (ed). The influence of economic evaluation studies on health care decision making: a European survey. Amsterdam: IOS Press.

Hardens et al. (1994), Poster, Pharmacoeconomic Conference, Ghent, Belgium, May

Henriksson F, Fredrikson S, Masterman T, Jönsson B (2001). Costs, quality of life and disease severity in multiple sclerosis. A cross-sectional study in Sweden. European Journal of Neurology 8:27-35.

Henriksson F, Jönsson B (1998). The economic cost of multiple sclerosis in Sweden in 1994. PharmacoEconomics 13(5Pt2):597-606.

van Hout B A, Al M J, Gordon G S, Rutten F F H (1994). Cost, effects and C/E-ratios alongside a clinical trial. Health Economics 3: 309-319.

International Monetary Fund (2001). World Economic Outlook. Washington: International Monetary Fund.

Johannesson M, Jönsson B (1991). Economic evaluation in health care: is there a role for cost-benefit analysis? Health Policy 17(1):1-23.

Johannesson M, Meltzer D, O'Conor R M (1997). Incorporating future costs in medical cost-effectiveness analysis: implications for the cost-effectiveness of the treatment of hypertension. Medical Decision Making 17(4):382-9.

Johannesson M, O'Conor R M, Kobelt G, Mattiasson A (1997). Willingness to pay for reduced incontinence symptoms. British Journal of Urology 80:557-562.

Jönsson B, Karlsson G (1990). Economic evaluation of cancer treatments. ESO monographs. Springer Verlag.

Jönsson B, Krieglstein G (eds) (1998). Primary-open angle glaucoma. Differences in international treatment patterns and cost. Isis Medical Media, Oxford, UK.

Kartman B, Andersson F, Johannesson M (1996). Willingness to pay for reductions in angina pectoris attacks. Medical Decision Making 16(3):248-53.

Kobelt G, Gerdtham UG, Alm A (1998). Costs of treating primary open angle glaucoma. Journal of Glaucoma, 7, 95-104.

Kobelt G, Jönsson L (1999) Modelling cost of patient management with new topical treatments for glaucoma. Results for France and the UK. International Journal of Technology Assessment in Health Care 15(1): 207-219.

Kobelt, G, Jönsson L, Eberhardt K, Jönsson B (1999). Economic consequences of the progression of rheumatoid arthritis in Sweden. Arthritis And Rheumatism 42(2): 347-56.

Kobelt G, Jönsson L, Fredriksson S, Jönsson B (2001). Cost-utility analysis of interferon beta-1b in the treatment of different types of multiple sclerosis. SSE/EFI Working Paper in Economics and Finance No. 459, August, Stockholm School of Economics, Stockholm.

Kobelt G, Jönsson L, Gerdtham U, Krieglstein G K (1998). Direct costs of glaucoma management following initiation of medical therapy. A simulation model based on an observational study of glaucoma treatment in Germany. Graefe's Archive for Clinical and Experimental Ophthalmology 236(11):811-21.

Kobelt G, Jönsson L, Henriksson F, Fredrikson S, Jönsson B (2000). Cost-utility of interferon beta-1b in secondary progressive multiple sclerosis. International Journal of Technology Assessment in Health Care 16(3):768-780.

Kobelt G, Jönsson L, Lindgren P, Eberhardt K, Young A. The cost-effectiveness of infliximab in the treatment of rheumatoid arthritis in Sweden and the United Kingdom, based on the ATTRACT trial. (forthcoming, British Journal of Rheumatology).

Kobelt G, Jönsson L, Lindgren P, Eberhardt K, Young A. Economic progression of rheumatoid arthritis in Sweden and in the United Kingdom. (Forthcoming, Arthritis and Rheumatism).

Kobelt G, Jönsson L, Miltenburger C (2002). Cost-utility analysis of interferon beta-1b in secondary progressive multiple sclerosis using natural history disease data. International Journal of Technology Assessment in Health Care 18(1):127-138.

Kobelt G, Lindgren P, Parkin D, Francis D A, Johnson M, Bates D, Jönsson B (2000). Costs and quality of life in multiple sclerosis. A cross-sectional observational study in the UK. SSE/EFI Working Paper in Economics and Finance No. 398. Stockholm: Stockholm School of Economics.

Kobelt G, Lindgren P, Smala A, Bitsch A, Haupts, Kölmel H W, König N, Rieckmann, Zettlthe U K, German Cost of MS Study Group (2001). Costs and quality of life in multiple sclerosis. An observational study in Germany. Health Economics in Prevention and Care 2(2): 60-68.

Kobelt G, Lindgren P, Smala A, Jönsson B (2000). Costs and quality of life in multiple sclerosis. A cross-sectional observational study in Germany. SSE/EFI Working Paper in Economics and Finance No. 399. Stockholm: Stockholm School of Economics.

Koopmanschap M A, Rutten F F H, van Ineveld B M, van Roijen L (1995). The friction cost method for measuring indirect costs of disease. Journal of Health Economics 14: 171-189.

Lindgren B (1990). The economic impact of illness. In: Costs of Illness and Benefits of Drug Treatment, Abshagen.

Lubitz J, Beebe J, Baker C (1995). Longevity and Medicare expenditures. New England Journal of Medicine 332(15):999-1003.

Luce B R, Manning W G, Siegel J E, Lipscomb J (1996). Estimating costs in cost-effectiveness analysis. In Gold M R, Siegel J E, Russell L B, Weinstein M C (eds), Cost-Effectiveness in Health and Medicine. New York: Oxford University Press.

Maynard A (1991). Developing the healthcare market. The Economic Journal 101:1277-1286.

Meltzer D (1997). Accounting for future costs in medical cost-effectiveness analysis. Journal of Health Economics 16(1):33-64.

National Institute for Clinical Excellence (2000). Framework Document. London: National Institute for Clinical Excellence.

National Institute for Clinical Excellence (2001). Guidance for manufacturers and sponsors. London: National Institute for Clinical Excellence (one of five documents advising on the appraisal process, the latest versions of which are available on the NICE website www.nice.org.uk).

O'Brien B J, Drummond M F, Labelle R J, Willan A (1994). In search of power and significance: issues in the design and analysis of stochastic cost-effectiveness studies in health care. Medical Care 32(2):150-63.

Office of Health Economics (2001). Health Economic Evaluations Database (HEED). London: Office of Health Economics.

Organisation for Economic Cooperation and Development (2001). OECD Health Data 2001. A comparative analysis of 30 countries. Paris: Organisation for Economic Cooperation and Development.

Sculpher M, Fenwick E, Claxton K (2000). Assessing quality in decision analytic cost-effectiveness models: a suggested framework and example of application. PharmacoEconomics 17(5):461-477.

Stalmeier P F M, Chapman G B, de Boer A G E M, van Lanschot J J B (2001). A fallacy of the multiplicative QALY model for low-quality weights in students and patients judging hypothetical health states. International Journal of Technology Assessment in Health Care 17(4): 488-496.

Swedberg K, Kjekshus J, Snapinn S, for the consensus investigators (1999). Long term survival in severe heart failure patients treated with enalapril. European Heart Journal 20:136-139.

Task Force on Principles for Economic Analysis of Health Care Technology (1995). Economic analysis of health care technology. A report on principles. Annals of Internal Medicine 123(1):61-70.

Torrance G W, Feeny D H, Furlong W J, Barr R D (1996). Multiattribute utility function for a comprehensive health status classification system: Health Utilities Index Mark 2. Medical Care 34;702-722.

Upmeier H, Miltenburger C. The cost of MS in Germany: a top-down analysis. ISTAHC 2000, Den Haag, 18-21 June.

Wakker P, Klaassen M P (1995). Confidence intervals for cost/effectiveness ratios. Health Economics 4(5):373-81.

Willke R J, Glick H A, Polsky D, Schulman K (1998). Estimating country-specific cost-effectiveness from multinational clinical trials. Health Economics 7: 481-493.

Zethraeus N, Johannesson M, Jönsson B (1999). A computer model to analyze the cost-effectiveness of hormone replacement therapy. International Journal of Technology Assessment in Health Care 15(2): 352-365.

7 Glossary

Average cost
: Total cost of therapy divided by the total quantity of treatment units provided.

Bayesian analysis
: An approach to statistical analysis which allows prior evidence and beliefs to be incorporated formally into the analysis of new data.

Bootstrapping
: A technique which involves resampling with replacement of patient data from an existing data set. By performing multiple repetitions (1000 or more) of this procedure, simulated distributions of variables of interest, such as mean costs, mean effects and the incremental cost-effectiveness ratio (ICER) can be derived. Uncertainty around these statistics can then be explored without making assumptions about their distribution.

Burden/cost of illness study
: A descriptive study that relates direct and indirect costs to a defined illness.

Confidence interval
: A range of values which contains the true value of the variable of interest a given percentage (e.g. 95%) of the time in repeated sampling.

Contingent valuation
: A method of eliciting individuals' preferences for a service by asking how much they are hypothetically willing to pay for the service. It is the technique conventionally used to obtain attach monetary values to the benefits of health care in cost-benefit analysis.

Cost-benefit analysis
: Type of economic evaluation that measures costs and benefits in monetary units and computes a net pecuniary gain/loss.

Cost-effectiveness
: Efficient use of (scarce) resources.

Cost-effectiveness acceptability curve
: A line showing the proportion of estimates of the ICER falling below the threshold ICER for different values of the threshold, frequently interpreted as the probability that the intervention is cost-effective.

Cost-effectiveness analysis
: Type of economic evaluation that measures therapeutic effects in physical or natural units and computes a cost/effectiveness ratio for comparison purposes.

Cost-minimization analysis	Type of economic evaluation that finds the lowest cost programme among those shown to be of equal benefit.
Cost-utility analysis	Type of analysis that measures therapeutic consequences in utility units (e.g. QALYs) rather than in physical units.
DALY	The Disability-Adjusted Life Year, a measure akin to the QALY in aggregating survival and quality of life effects but normally advanced as a method of estimating the burden of illness associated with a disease, rather than the cost-effectiveness of health care interventions.
Decision analysis	An explicit quantitative approach to decision-making under uncertainty, with a structure designed to represent the treatment options under investigation and normally based on a synthesis of data from the literature.
Direct medical costs	Fixed and variable costs associated directly with a health care intervention.
Direct non-medical costs	Non-medical costs associated with provision of medical services.
Discounting	The adjustment of future costs and benefits to render those occurring in different years comparable with each other and with current costs and benefits. The adjustment operates in the opposite way to compound interest, i.e. a positive discount rate weights the future less than the present.
Disease management	A health care management process bringing together the development and delivery of all health care interventions and costs relevant to the prevention and management of a particular disease.
Economic evaluation	A comparative analysis of two or more alternatives in terms of their costs and consequences.
Effectiveness	The therapeutic consequence of a treatment in a real world conditions.
Efficacy	The consequence (benefit) of a treatment under ideal and controlled clinical conditions, for example in a clinical trial.

Health economics	Application of the theories, concepts and tools of economics to the topic of health and health care.
Health-related quality of life	The impact on an individual's well-being of their health, often encompassing physical, mental and psychosocial elements.
Health state	A summary description of an individual's health-related quality of life.
HYE	The Healthy Years Equivalent, a summary measure of health outcome analogous to the QALY in combining survival with quality of life, derived using a two-stage standard gamble technique.
Incremental cost	The additional cost that one service or programme imposes over another, mutually exclusive, alternative.
Incremental cost-effectiveness ratio (ICER)	The additional cost of producing an extra unit of outcome by one therapy compared with another.
Indirect costs/ productivity costs	Cost of reduced productivity resulting from illness or treatment.
Intangible costs	The cost of pain and suffering as a result of illness or treatment.
Marginal cost	The extra cost of one extra unit of product or service delivered.
Markov analysis	A modelling technique to handle decision problems involving risks that are potentially continuously variable over time and where the timing of the events is important.
Meta-analysis	A systematic process for finding, evaluating and combining the results of sets of data from different scientific studies.
Moral hazard	A change in behaviour of buyers or sellers as a result of insurance. Insurance changes behaviour because it alters the level of risk faced by the buyers and sellers.
Net benefit (NB)	A summary measure of the difference between an intervention's mean incremental health effects (ΔE, normally measured in QALYs) and its mean

incremental costs (ΔC) relative to an alternative. The incremental NB can be expressed in monetary terms (the money value of ΔE minus ΔC) or, less frequently, health terms. A positive NB implies that the ICER is within the threshold ICER.

Opportunity cost	The benefit forgone from using a resource for one purpose as opposed to its best alternative use.
Outcomes research	The study of the ultimate therapeutic consequences of a treatment, including its effect on patients' quality of life.
Pharmacoeconomics	The economic evaluation of pharmaceutical products.
Probabilistic sensitivity analysis	A technique used to explore the impact on a simulated group of patients (such as those entered into a Markov model) of uncertainty around estimates of the input parameters.
QALY	The Quality-Adjusted Life Year is the outcome of a treatment measured as the number of years of life saved, adjusted for their utility (quality of life).
Sensitivity analysis	The assessment of the robustness of study results through systematic variation of key variables.
Standard gamble	A method of valuing health states on a 0-1 scale by presenting individuals with a choice between a given health state for certain and a gamble offering (for better than death states) outcomes of death (valued as 0) and perfect health (1). The probability of perfect health at which the individual would be indifferent between the two options gives the value of the health state.
Threshold ICER	The maximum willingness to pay for health benefits, normally expressed as the maximum cost per QALY that decision makers consider acceptable for a health care intervention.
Time trade-off	A means of valuing health states on a 0-1 scale by asking individuals how many years in perfect health are equivalent to a given number of years in a less than perfect health state. Years in perfect health divided by years in the defined health state gives the value for that health state.

Utility   A measure of the relative preference for, or desirability of, a specific level of health status or a specific health outcome.

Visual analogue scale   A means of valuing health states on a 0-1 scale by asking individuals to place them on a line ranging from best possible health (valued as 1) to worst possible health/death (0).

8 Further reading

General Health Economics and the Economic Evaluation of Health Care

Drummond MF, O'Brien B, Stoddart GL, Torrance GW.
Methods for the Economic Evaluation of Health Care Programmes 2nd edition.
Oxford: Oxford Medical Publications, 1997.

Folland S, Goodman AC, Stano M.
The Economics of Health and Health Care.
Oxford: Maxwell MacMillan International, 1993.

Gold M R, Siegel J E, Russell L B, Weinstein M C.
Cost-Effectiveness in Health and Medicine.
New York: Oxford University Press, 1996.

Johannesson M.
Theory and methods of economic evaluation of health care.
Dordrecht: Kluwer Academic Publishers, 1996.

Phelps CE.
Health Economics.
New York: Harper Collins Publishers Inc, 1992.

Sloan F A (ed).
Valuing Health Care: costs, benefits and effectiveness of pharmaceuticals and other medical technologies.
New York: Cambridge University Press, 1995.

Confidence Intervals for Cost-effectiveness Ratios

Briggs A H, Mooney C Z, Wonderling D E.
Constructing confidence intervals for cost-effectiveness ratios: an evaluation of parametric and non-parametric techniques using Monte Carlo simulation.
Statistics in Medicine, 1999; 18:3245-3262.

Briggs A H, Wonderling D E, Mooney C Z.
Pulling cost-effectiveness analysis up by its bootstraps: a non-parametric approach to confidence interval estimation.
Health Economics, 1997; 6:327-340.

Polsky D, Glick H A, Willke R, Schulman K.
Confidence intervals for cost-effectiveness ratios: a comparison of four methods.
Health Economics, 1997; 6:243-252.

Tambour M, Zethraeus N (1998). Bootstrap confidence intervals for cost-effectiveenss ratios: some simulation results. Health Economics 7: 143-147.

Wakker P, Klaassen MP.
Confidence intervals for cost-effectiveness ratios.
Health Economics, 1995; 4:373-381.

Cost-effectiveness Acceptability Curves:

Briggs A, Fenn P.
Confidence intervals or surfaces? Uncertainty on the cost-effectiveness plane.
Health Economics, 1998; 7:723-740.

Fenwick E, Claxton K, Sculpher M.
Representing uncertainty: the role of cost-effectiveness acceptability curves.
Health Economics, 2001; 10:779-787.

Van Hout B A, Al M J, Gordon G S, Rutten F F H.
Costs, effects and c-e ratios alongside a clinical trial.
Health Economics, 1994; 3:309-319.

Lothgren M, Zethraeus N.
Definition, interpretation and calculation of cost-effectiveness acceptability curves.
Health Economics, 2000; 9:623-630.

Costs

Briggs A, Gray A.
The distribution of health care costs and their statistical analysis for economic evaluation.
Journal of Health Services Research and Policy, 1998; 3(4):233-245.

Desgagne A, Castilloux A-M, Angers J-F, LeLorier J.
The use of the bootstrap statistical method for the pharmacoeconomic cost analysis of skewed data.
PharmacoEconomics, 1998; 13(5pt1):487-497.

Luce BR, Elixhauser A.
Estimating Costs in Economic Evaluation of Medical Technologies.
International Journal of Technology Assessment in Health Care, 1990; 6:57-75.

Decision Analysis

Keeney RL, Raiffa H.
Decisions With Multiple Objectives: preferences and value tradeoffs.
New York: John Wiley and Sons, 1976.

Rittenhouse B.
Uses of models in economic evaluations of medicines and other health technologies.
London: Office of Health Economics, 1996.

Sculpher M, Fenwick E, Claxton K.
Assessing quality in decision analytic cost-effectiveness models: a suggested framework and example of application.
PharmacoEconomics, 2000; 17(5):461-477.

Tom E, Schulman K A.
Mathematical models in decision analysis.
Infection Control and Hospital Epidemiology, 1997; 18:65-73.

Weinstein MC.
Principles of Cost-effective resource allocation in health care organisations.
International Journal of Technology Assessment in Health Care, 1990; 6:93-103.

Discounting

Brouwer W, van Hout B, Rutten F F H.
A fair approach to discounting future effects: taking a societal perspective.
Journal of Health Services Research and Policy, 2000; 5(2):114-118.

Coyle D, Tolley K.
Discounting of health benefits in the pharmacoeconomic analysis of drug therapies. An issue for debate?
PharmacoEconomics, 1992; 2(2):153-162.

Van Hout B A.
Discounting costs and effects: a reconsideration.
Health Economics, 1998; 7:581-594.

Krahn M, Gafni A.
Discounting in the economic evaluation of health care interventions.
Medical Care, 1993; 31:403-418.

Smith D H, Gravelle H.
The practice of discounting in economic evaluations of healthcare interventions.
International Journal of Technology Assessment in Health Care, 2001; 17(2):236-243.

Economic Evaluation in Clinical Practice

Eisenberg JM.
Clinical Economics: A Guide to the Economic Analysis of Clinical Practices.
Journal of the American Medical Association, 1989; 262(20):2879-2886.

Weinstein MC.
Economic Assessment of Medical Practices and Technologies.
Medical Decision Making, 1981; 1(4):309-330.

Guidelines for Economic Evaluation

Alban A, Keiding H, Søgaard (1998). Guidelines for economic evaluations of pharmaceuticals. Copenhagen: Danish Ministry of Health.

Collège des Economistes de la Santé (1997). Guidelines and recommendations for French pharmaco-economic studies. La Lettre du Collège numero special: evaluation for French pharmaco-economic studies.

Garattini L, Grilli R, Scopelliti D, Mantovani L (1995). A proposal for Italian guidelines in pharmacoeconomics. PharmacoEconomics 7(1):1-6.

Hannoveraner Konsensus Gruppe (1999). Deutsche Empfehlungen zur gesundheitsoekonomischen Evaluation -Revidierte Fassung des Hannoveraner Konsens. Gesundheitsoekonomie und Qualitaetsmanagement 4 A62 - A65.

Italian Group for Pharmacoeconomic Studies (1997). Pharmecoeconomic studies: Italian proposal for guidelines. Pavia: University of Pavia.

Langley P C (1998). Guidelines for formulary submissions for pharmaceutical product evaluation. Blue Cross Blue Shield of Colorado, Blue Cross Blue Shield of Nevada.

Ministry of Health (1994). Ontario guidelines for economic analysis of pharmaceutical products. Toronto: Ministry of Health.

Ministry of Social Affairs and Health (1999). Guidelines for preparation of an account of health-economic aspects. Helsinki: Ministry of Social Affairs and Health.

Norwegian Medicines Agency (2000). Norwegian guidelines for pharmacoeconomic analysis in connection with applications for reimbursement. Oslo: Norwegian Medicines Agency.

Pharmaceutical Management Agency Ltd (1999). A prescription for pharmacoeconomic analysis. Wellington: Pharmac.

Rovira J, Antonanzas F (2001). Propuesta de estandarizacion de algunos aspectos metodologicos de los analisis coste-efectividad y coste-utilidad en la evaluacion de tecnologias y programmeas sanitarios. http://www.farmacoeconomia.com/Directrices/spespana.htm.

Da Silva E A, Pinto C G, Sampaio C, Pereira J A, Drummond M, Trindade R (1998). Methodological guidelines for economic evaluation studies for drugs. Lisbon.

Sickness Funds Council (1999). Dutch guidelines for pharmacoeconomic research. Amstelveen: Ziekenfondsraad.

Markov Analysis

Briggs A, Sculpher M
An introduction to Markov modelling for economic evaluation
Pharmacoeconomics, 1999; 13(4):397-409.

Hunink M G M, Bult J, DeVries J, Weinstein M C.
Uncertainty in cost-effectiveness analysis evaluated with a non-parametric bootstrap method: combining first and second-order monte-carlo simulation of a Markov model.
Medical Decision Making, 1997; 17(4):536

Sonnenberg PA, Beck JR.
Markov Models in Medical Decision Making: Practical Guide.
Medical Decision Making, 1993; 13:322-328.

Net Benefits

Briggs A H.
A Bayesian approach to stochastic cost-effectiveness analysis.
International Journal of Technology Assessment in Health Care, 2001; 17(1):69-82.

Laska E M, Meisner M, Siegel C, Stinnett A A.
Ratio-based and net benefit-based approaches to health care resource allocation: proofs of optimality and equivalence.
Health Economics, 1999; 8:171-174.

Stinnett A A, Mullahy J A.
Net health benefits: a new framework for the analysis of uncertainty in cost-effectiveness analysis.
Medical Decision Making, 1998; 18(2suppl):S68-S80.

Quality of Life

Guyatt GW, Feeny JH, Patrick DL.
Measuring Health Related Quality of Life.
Annals of Internal Medicine, 1993; 118:622-629.

Spilker B (Ed).
Quality of Life and Pharmacoeconomics in Clinical Trials, 2nd Edition.
Philadelphia: Lippincott-Raven, 1996.

Walker SR, Rosser RM (Ed).
Quality of Life: Assessment and Application.
Lancaster: MTP Press Limited (Kluwer), 1987.

QALY League Tables

Chapman R H, Stone P W, Sandberg E A, Bell C, Neumann P J.
A comprehensive league table of cost-utility ratios and sub-table of "panel worthy" studies.
Medical Decision Making, 1999; 19(4):521.

Mason J M.
Cost-per-QALY league tables: their roles in pharmacoeconomic analysis.
PharmacoEconomics, 1994; 5(6): 472-481.

Mason J, Drummond M, Torrance G.
Some guidelines on the use of cost-effectiveness league tables.
British Medical Journal, 1993; 306:570-572.

Petrou S, Malek M, Davey P G.
The reliability of cost-utility estimates in cost-per-QALY league tables.
PharmacoEconomics, 1993; 3(5):345-353.

Sensitivity Analysis in Economic Evaluation

Briggs A.
Handling Uncertainty in the Results of Economic Evaluation.
Briefing No. 32, London: Office of Health Economics, 1995.

Briggs A H.
Handling uncertainty in cost-effectiveness models.
PharmacoEconomics, 2000; 17(5):479-500.

Briggs A, Sculpher M.
Sensitivity Analysis in Economic Evaluation.
Health Economics, 1995; 4:359-371.

Briggs A, Schulpher M, Buxton MJ.
Uncertainty in the Economic Evaluation of Health Care Technologies; the role of sensitivity analysis.
Health Economics, 1994; 3:95-104.

Statistics in Economic Evaluation

Briggs A H, Gray A M.
Power and sample size calculations for stochastic cost-effectiveness analysis.
Medical Decision Making, 1998; 18(Suppl):S81-S92.

Coyle D.
Statistical analysis in pharmacoeconomic studies: a review of current issues and standards.
PharmacoEconomics, 1996; 9(6):506-516.

O'Brien BJ, Drummond MF, Labelle RJ, Willan A.
In Search of Power and Significance. Issues in the Design and Analysis of Stochastic Cost-effectiveness Studies in Health Care.
Medical Care, 1994; 32(2):150-163.

Utility Assessment

Torrance GW.
Measurement of Health State Utilities For Economic Appraisal: A Review.
Journal of Health Economics, 1986; 5:1-30.

Williams A.
The measurement and valuation of health: a chronicle.
Discussion Paper 136.
University of York, 1995.

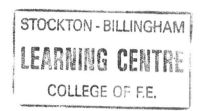

Willingness to Pay

Bala M V, Mauskopf J A, Wood L L.
Willingness to pay as a measure of health benefits.
PharmacoEconomics, 1999; 15(1):9-18

Johannesson M, Jönsson B.
Economic Evaluation in Health Care: is there a role for cost-benefit analysis?
Health Policy, 1991; 17:1-23.

Olsen J A, Smith R D.
Theory versus practice: a review of 'willingness-to-pay' in health and health care.
Health Economics, 2001; 10:39-52.